It's People That Count

It's People That Count

The Very Reverend Dr Andrew B. Doig

with a Foreword by

The Reverend Robert P Sloan

The Pentland Press Limited
Edinburgh • Cambridge • Durham • USA

© Andrew B. Doig 1997

First published in 1997 by
The Pentland Press Ltd.
1 Hutton Close
South Church
Bishop Auckland
Durham

British Library Cataloguing in Publication Data.
A catalogue record for this book is available
from the British Library.

ISBN 1 85821 482 3

Typeset by CBS, Felixstowe, Suffolk
Printed and bound by Antony Rowe Ltd., Chippenham

To my dear wife, Barbara
companion and helper
over so many years
and to our children,
Peter, Isabelle and Anne.

Contents

Foreword

I took this book on holiday with me in the autumn of 1996 and spent an enjoyable couple of hours discovering someone I had met on a number of occasions and felt I wanted to know better. I was not disappointed.

The following pages introduce you to the encounters of a far-travelled ambassador for Christ. From Trinity College, Glasgow, he went to Union Seminary, New York; from there to Africa as a missionary, i.e. designer of septic tanks, surveyor, estate manager and evangelist, Army Chaplain and, much to my surprise, a politician who was forthright and therefore at times unpopular during the legislative nightmares of Central Africa in the 1950s.

Andrew returned to Scotland to be Parish Minister, Presbytery Clerk, General Secretary of the National Bible Society of Scotland and in 1981 Moderator of the General Assembly.

At a service of ordination a minister is asked 'Do you engage in the strength of the Lord Jesus Christ to live a godly and circumspect life; and faithfully, diligently and cheerfully to discharge the duties of your ministry, seeking an all things the advancement of the Kingdom of God?' These chapters reveal how Andrew Doig kept that vow in a wide variety of appointments and assignments, pastoral and political, international and interdenominational, consistently believing that the people for whom any organisation exists are always more important than the organisation.

Andrew's energy and enthusiasm for the individual, his Christlikeness and humanity have touched the lives of many people. It is a great honour to write this introduction to a book about a man whose example is both an inspiration and a challenge.

The Rev. Robert P. Sloan, MA, BD
Minister of Braemar and Crathie and
Domestic Chaplain to Her Majesty the Queen

Preface

I am looking back over many years, but in this biographical exercise, I shall be careful to avoid being too detailed or dreamy or introspective. What grips me is the sense of continuity of purpose, the amazing way in which the experiences and lessons of each portion of my life and ministry were used and had prepared me for those that followed in such a deep and satisfying way that one can only say in deep humility – Thanks be to God.

There have been failures, moments of indecision, conflict of interests, doubts and even fears but I have been left in no doubt that there is a Providence that shapes our ends, rough hew them how we will. That shaping influence is no impersonal accident but the loving purpose of God in Christ Jesus. Moreover, all along the way, it has been people that were important, what they were and what they said and to what extent they heard and applied the Word of God.

A.B.D.

Illustrations

Chapter 1

Early Days

The First World War broke out as I was born. The second erupted as I set out for Africa as a missionary. Interpret that how you will, but it has always reminded me that I was in a real world and there was no easy way.

I was born in Carluke, Lanarkshire and baptised in St John's Church there, by the Rev Matthew Turnbull. I was to catch up with him later, much later, when in 1937, I did summer preaching in Wanlockhead where he spent the latter years of his ministry.

As a family, we left Carluke, when I was just 7 years old, but I have some impressive memories of the place. From the upstairs window of my grandmother's house, overlooking the Square, I recall watching the presentation of the Victoria Cross to a distinguished son of the town at the end of the First World War. I began school in Carluke and found pleasure in finding variant ways of making the considerable journey from home to school.

We left Carluke for Glasgow in 1921. There we stayed, first in Mount Florida, then in Hyndland and later in Knightswood.

I went straight from school to university and theological college, followed by postgraduate study at Union Theological Seminary in the United States and then off to begin my exciting service in Africa.

There are those today who place great stress on the importance of candidates for the ministry having experience of the world. All honour to those who have made their way in industry or commerce and feel the hand of God upon them to enter the ministry, but it is so wrong to assume that those going straight from school can have no meaningful knowledge of the world and of life, can have no powerful stimulus or considered judgement on the issues to which the Gospel must be applied. Certainly for those of us, brought up in the twenties and the thirties, as teenagers we learned the hard way about social conditions and proved the essential value of a warm home discipline and a shared life.

I saw my father bearing the scars in himself of unemployment. I saw my mother struggling to make ends meet as reserves and savings vanished. Yet I recall the sheer joy of simple holidays in Saltcoats and Arbroath, planned and shared by father, mother and the three boys. We knew that we shared pressures that other families faced. Ours was intensified when my father died in 1928 of tuberculosis and my mother remained the strength and inspiration of three boys, David aged 17, Andrew aged 14 and George aged 8.

I was asked in a TV interview in the year I became Moderator: 'What made you become a minister?' The ease with which words came to me, surprised me but even in subsequent recollection, I could not achieve a better reply. I said,

Firstly, in a congregation in Glasgow, Broomhill, we had a minister, Turner Kennedy by name, whose gracious personality and preaching expertise communicated powerfully to young people. Under that ministry, I knew and answered the call of God.

Secondly, there was the congregation, large in numbers and so varied in its make-up, extensive in organisations and activities, social and spiritual and missionary. In that fellowship, I played and learned and made a start in missionary outreach.

Thirdly, there was my home, a close-knit family of faith, in which it was a joy to be alive. Both father and mother had their own stories to tell of faith and vision. We were proud of my father, on the staff of the railway, who bore the marks of an accident suffered on duty, in which he lost an arm. His loss gave him heroic stature in the eyes of his sons. His gifts were many and most noticeable was his ability as a tenor soloist. What a disappointment it must have been to him when I returned from an audition with the Junior Orpheus Choir to confess I had failed to make the grade. Yet he was quick to respond hopefully – 'There must be other gifts you are meant to develop'. That was his challenge to me, which I often thought of as the years passed.

My mother was the daughter of a writer and newspaper publisher in Carluke, Andrew Beveridge. He started the *Carluke and Lanark Gazette*. Playing around the printing office, perhaps I got a sense of the power and imperative of communication. However, the direction and issue of communication for me was most determined by the fact that my mother, as a young woman, had a dream to be a missionary in Livingstonia. That dream could not be fulfilled because of the demands of the family business but what a joy it was for her to see me setting forth on a path she had never been able to travel.

These three factors in formative years came together in a special way, when, after father died, it seemed that we boys would have to find paid employment as soon as possible and give up all thought of a university education. The minister and congregation of Broomhill would not have it so. Gracious generous people, who never allowed their names to be known to us provided the support and finance that opened up for our family new possibilities.

Education and Early Outreach in Mission

I was fortunate to enjoy a happy schooling in Glasgow. It was a long way from Knightswood to Hyndland every day but the school was a hive of varied activity and some choice personalities. I was secretary to the Literary and Debating Society, concentrated on Classics in my upper forms and ventured forth on the rugby field and running track. In my first game for the 1st XV, I broke my big toe, which ended my rugby career and laid me up for some time in my sixth year. The advantage was plenty of time for study and the gaining of a bursary in the University Open Bursary Competition.

My favourite character among the school staff was Duncan Anderson, our English master. I owe so much to him in his introduction of me to the treasures of English Literature. He was a small man in stature but equipped with a voice that could be heard all over the school. He described this contrast between stature and voice as the divine law of compensation. Often, I have encouraged myself and others in any limiting situation to let that law work.

At university I had most of my Arts subjects in the Classics and in Mathematics. Perhaps in the light of my later involvement overseas, I would have benefitted from some freedom in linguistics but Classics and Mathematics are a grand foundation for further study and a disciplined life.

Theological college was a joy to me. I was following in the footsteps of my brother, David. It was a great day when Mother saw David and myself capped at the same ceremony in the Bute Hall, BD and MA respectively. I owe a lot to my brother, who carried the heavier load in helping the family finances by having a full-time assistantship all through his theological course. Nevertheless, he excelled in his studies as well and I had a hard act to follow.

I was given the opportunity to engage in a variety of avenues of Christian service – in Sunday School teaching, in addressing Band of

Hope meetings and especially under the inspiration and leadership of the Church of Scotland evangelist, D.P. Thomson in the mission outreaches of the mid and late 1930s. I was assistant to 'D.P.' as he is fondly remembered, in 1936 for two months in the Summer Missions at Prestwick, Troon and Ayr. Nothing was impossible in D.P.'s reckoning, be it stripping the harmonium which had become clogged with sand or hoisting a screen for open air projection on the front at Troon, where every moment I expected it to take off for Arran in the strong breeze blowing.

The student participation in Summer Mission led us to see possibilities of campaigns at such times as Easter. We formed the Glasgow Student Campaigners. I had the joy of being appointed the first leader. We had two ventures – in 1937 at Strathaven and Stonehouse (where my elder brother, David, was now minister) and

The Doigs; graduated at same ceremony standing (left) Andrew MA and (right) David BD with George and Mother.

5

in 1938 at Port Glasgow. One feature of these campaigns from Trinity College, was that our professors came with us. I have vivid memories of a large lunch-time rally at the shipyard gates in Port Glasgow. The men stood around in great numbers listening to Professors Gossip or Mauchline or Riddell on our portable platform. They asked them searching questions and we admired the way the speakers handled them. The constant interest and participation of the staff strengthened our fellowship, gave new depth to our vision and was a powerful and practical extension of our theological studies.

The names mentioned above are but a few of the professors who influenced me greatly at university and Trinity College. McNeil Dixon guided me in philosophy, Rennie and Davies grounded me in the Classics. I have a vivid and thankful remembrance of the devotional and pastoral talks given by Principal W.M. Macgregor in the divinity hall. My specialist studies for the degree of BD were in New Testament and I am eternally grateful for the scholarship and communications expertise of Garth Macgregor.

We had the doubtful distinction of being the largest year that ever passed through Trinity College – seventy men and one woman. So we called ourselves the Gadholian Club (Hebrew for great). We came from varied backgrounds and covered a fair age range. We had a happy college life, sharing in many activities – not least in the table tennis room up the tower. I held the championship for quite some time – the only championship I ever held in my life.

I have followed with interest the contribution made by men of our year to the Church. Ludovic Gray and Andrew Maclellan (the two colonels we called them), two effective parish ministers; George Docherty who went on to distinguish himself in the New York Avenue Presbyterian Church in Washington, USA and act as Chaplain to the American Senate; George Johnston, academically easily first in our year, who entered on an effective teaching career in Theology and

New Testament in Canada; and Jim Reid, my special friend in College and in America, who was to exercise a notable ministry in Forfar and Broughty Ferry.

We all rejoiced to meet on the golf course. I built up a set of clubs that cost me seven shillings and sixpence (thirty-five new pence) per club. They were to serve me well for many years until in the 1970s, my son Peter, who was developing fast in reducing his handicap, pointed out to me that it was really time I bought myself some new clubs as these old ones had now cost me about one penny each year over the years. I gave in and replaced them.

At the end of my course in 1938, I was awarded one of the two scholarships for Union Theological Seminary in New York. My partner in discovery was George Balls from St Andrews. We fitted well together and had a great time, keeping fit in the gymnasium of Riverside Church, travelling our separate ways according to our choice in vacations and putting together our experiences to contribute as a Scottish team to the life of Union. We roamed the haunts of Harlem and ventured up into the New England States to join Jim Reid who was enjoying a scholarship there. In Union Seminary, I had the great joy of sitting at the feet of Niebuhr and Tillich, so greatly benefitting from the brilliance of their exposition.

I was already ordained and accepted as a missionary of the Church of Scotland and so my studies and travels in the United States took that into account. I took as the subject of my thesis for the STM degree – 'The Missionary Motive and the Missionary Approach in the light of the fundamentals of the Christian Faith'. What rash self-confidence – but at 23 years of age, there are no limits to the expectations one has of oneself!

In company with George Molefe, a jovial black minister from South Africa, I travelled widely in the Southern States. We rejoiced in the exciting volume of singing in the Negro College at Hampton, Virginia and learned at first hand the difficulties of inter-racial living at that time in the States. Though I did not realise it, this was to become an urgent concern of mine in years to come.

Chapter 2

Africa – Here I Come

All along in the USA, my thought was of going to Africa. My course in education, my contacts, my degree, all had this significance.

I returned through Canada, my stay there being far shorter than hoped for, because of the demand from 121 George Street that I hasten to prepare for service in Africa, in Nyasaland, where a resignation had left them short staffed.

My return was to witness the war clouds gathering and then came the outbreak of war in September 1939. I made a journey to Edinburgh to suggest that I had better get into action at this end than appear to isolate myself out there. Dr Kydd, the Overseas Secretary, pleaded with me, saying, 'You are needed out there. The war will not touch it. The work must go on.'

I was not really convinced but I went out later that month. I was soon immersed in district work, gathering some language skill and making innumerable friends in the church very speedily.

There was a tremendous variety in the missionary's life. I had always been keen on doing things with my hands and soon found plenty opportunities. I was given charge of the Naming'aazi Estate, between Zomba and Domasi, a fair expanse of garden land, on which we grew lots of vegetables, pineapples and other produce. I say I was in charge but the steady work and knowledgable planning was done by African colleagues.

Sanitation on Zomba station left something to be desired. I set myself to the task of building a septic tank. It was gloriously successful and when I returned years later, I was thrilled to find it still in use.

I spent a lot of time with another African craftsman, our station carpenter. He taught me the skills and so carpentry has remained my hobby ever since. Taking a lively interest in the construction of buildings, I was responsible for laying the plans for a new church in the Zomba district. I camped out at the site for a few days, got agreement as to which way the church was to face and marked out the lines for walls. Then I left them to get on with it, returning weeks later to behold the results. They were staggering. My good friends and parishioners had decided that the lines drawn on the ground made the church look far too small. They assumed that the new and very young missionary probably didn't know very much about building (in that they were correct) and so they re-drew the lines for the walls, dug the foundations and set to work. When I revisited, the walls were rising and I knew at once there was no way I could make a roof to span the gap. At the end of the day, I had to have pillars constructed down the centre of the church, to feed in the roof supports from both sides.

The African minister at Zomba was Harry Mtuwa, a man whom I remember with deep affection. He was firm in his views, compassionate and concerned for the spiritual needs of all. He pointed me on a firm course of caring for the individual. This was the more necessary as we were dealing with large numbers in Zomba Church. I well remember the day when I found myself with fifty-one babies to baptise, quite an undertaking, though joyful in the extreme. It had occurred to me that the full service would take a considerable time. I had an idea. Why should I not baptise each child and then pronounce one blessing over them all. It would greatly solve the time problem.

I put forward my idea to Harry Mtuwa. It was short lived, as he looked at me kindly but firmly and said, 'To each child an individual blessing.' I have never forgotten it. He was absolutely right. It is the essence of the Gospel, the promise of all preaching and therefore the sign of the Sacrament – to each an individual blessing.

I enjoyed my district work. I was officially missionary in charge of Zomba and Domasi districts. There were six African ministers, with whom I was associated, but I never considered myself in charge of them. We were a happy team. At the end of each month, we met in Zomba in the office and in my manse and planned ahead. I travelled widely through the forty-odd churches and prayerhouses. The many churches on the plain were a delight. Then there was the climb up the Domasi valley to what had been the old mission station.

Domasi was the third station to be opened in the early days and must have been a thriving centre. As the population moved down from the hills, it lost its importance but the old church remains a notable place of worship. It is a large brick building, well furnished and with a tiled floor. The chancel was impressive and all the way

On the bike.

down the church there were hung great oil lamps, which had been brought out from Scotland. Domasi was the end of the road but way up the valley, to be reached on foot, was another church, Kasonga, with a thriving congregation. You just kept on climbing, slowly and steadily and the welcome was always assured.

To the north of the Zomba-Domasi district lay Chiuta, a fascinating area with a widely scattered population, two churches and many prayerhouses. Nguru was the language used here. I travelled this extensive area of Zomba-Domasi and Ciuta with Thomas Price, missionary teacher and my tutor in the Chinyanja language. We visited churches and schools, heard and sorted out their problems and encouraged the workers. We camped out and the evenings were wonderful as we gathered with many others around the camp fire, talked and sang and had worship together.

Tom was a great companion. We shared a common university background, though of course, he left Glasgow ten years before I did. As a language teacher he was first class, thorough and demanding. He was widely recognised in linguistic circles as an expert. He produced a manual on the elements of Nyanja and tried it out on me chapter by chapter. I joked about it, suggesting it must be on the assumption that if I could learn from it, anyone could. One day I said to him that when I was searching for a word in Chinyanja, I would find a French word coming to mind. His comment was devastating but true and spoken with a twinkle in the eye. 'It could be,' said Tom, 'that you know neither language.' Of course, he was right.

When I was not with Tom in his car, I sallied forth on my great pride and joy, my BSA 500 motor cycle, with so much to learn. I had never been on a push bike in my entire life and here I was venturing to ride a fairly powerful motor bike, getting on well, when, as they say, pride goes before a fall. I set off for Blantyre, the main mission station, over forty miles away, to attend my first Presbytery meeting. Just six miles out of Zomba, I struck a very soft patch on the dirt road, skidded and mounted the bank at the side of the road. The bike came over on top of me and the result was a very severely damaged chin. I did a first aid job on myself and carried on to Blantyre where I had to have several stitches put in the chin by our good friend, Dr W.O. Petrie at our mission hospital. So I appeared, the new young missionary, eager to make a good impression, looking very much the worse for wear. At least it made me the centre of attraction and gave me a personal talking point.

I was delighted with the liveliness of the Church as I saw it at worship and in action throughout the district. There were so many churches and prayerhouses to be given leadership that the ordained staff by themselves could not cope. I had often heard in Scotland appeals for the greater involvement of the elders and the laity in the worship and teaching ministry of the Church. The response to such appeals often fell far short of the mark. Here in Nyasaland, I found it actually happening. There was an evangelist in every main church. They were men of varying age and ability but each was crucial to the development of the Church.

Once a year, we had an evangelists' course. There, along with some of the African ministers, I had the chance to teach them, to encourage them, to promote their Bible study and to guide them in a scheme of instruction they could apply in their congregation. They were natural in their conduct of public worship. I found it impressive and agreed with the Anglican missionary who was reflecting on the freedom our lay leaders showed in this regard. He said, 'There can be no doubt that it stems from their being steeped in the Word of God. So they come naturally into the Lord's presence and pour out their hearts not only in the spirit but in the very letter of God's Word.' I say Amen to that.

Singing was a great feature of the services and we were blessed with a great Hymn-book, in Chinyanja, Nyimbo za Mulungu. Many were translations of hymns, well known to us in English, suitably adapted, but others were the product of the faith of local people, set to African tunes. They were popular and compelling.

I have mentioned my love of Ciuta. One other favourite spot was the island of Mcisi, in Lake Chirwa, where there was a lively congregation. It was fun to cross to the island in a dug-out canoe on a bright sunny morning. There was a large deposit of tin on the island, the licence for the exploration of which was held by the Rio Tinto Mining Corporation. They have never yet exploited the resources. Perhaps we were lucky in Nyasaland that the mineral deposits were few, and so the agricultural opportunities held hope and life and income for the population.

Fulfilment was also found in the worship in English on a Sunday afternoon in Zomba Church. Those attending were mostly civil servants (Zomba being at that time the capital of Nyasaland) planters and staff of some of the commercial concerns, working in the area, like the famous African Lakes Corporation or Mandala. Increasingly, the congregation became multi-racial as a considerable number of Africans associated themselves with the afternoon service.

I met the Europeans also in the Zomba Club, a gracious friendly place with many sporting opportunities, few of which I was able to indulge in as games were mainly on Sundays. I did play for a short time on the wing of a hockey team and enjoyed the small golf course. One hole of the golf course passed our church, which explains why its windows had to be protected by wire netting.

The headquarters of the Army were in Zomba and I soon found myself involved with the chaplaincy work at the depot. Armies had never been much in my line, from the pacifist days of my youth but it was a happy link that I made with the depot at Zomba. I was very conscious of the distinguished story of the King's African Rifles, since the days of the Ashanti wars in the last century, but little did I think how I would become personally involved in the next chapter of their activities.

Another responsibility was that I was one of the chaplains to the Central Prison at Zomba. I still remember one man I visited through the period of his trial for murder. He grew upon me. We shared long talks about faith and fellowship, with constant use of the Bible. He was found guilty and sentenced to hang. I found it difficult to accept. I felt I knew him better than anyone else in the motive and hopes of his life. I did not believe he was guilty as convicted but there was little I could do. My visits became daily and then he made the unlooked for request that I should walk with him all the way from his cell to the place of execution. The doctor was also with us but he gave up, unable to face the last act. I felt sick, convinced I had been witnessing an injustice that there was no chance of changing. From that experience, I have remained ever since, a firm opponent of capital punishment. There are too many uncertainties in the process.

I have recalled with joy my special relationship with Harry Mtuwa. The other African minister with whom I developed a special link was Stephen Kundecha, a spare figure, large of heart and with a wide experience of the ministry. He was one of the first two ministers to be ordained in the Blantyre Synod. He was specially well versed in the whole question of our relationship with Islam. There were many Mohammedans in his area and he was most pertinent and active in his discussions with them. I caught the vision from him.

As the months passed, I had an urge to put an end to my bachelor status. On my return from the United States, I had become engaged to Nan Carruthers, also a member of the famous Broomhill Church. We had known each other for some years and the romance was an enriching experience. We could not go further than an engagement because of the rule of the Foreign Mission Committee that a missionary was supposed to be two years in service before he could become married. So I sailed alone in 1939. As 1940 developed I wrote asking Nan to brave the perilous seas in wartime, to join me and she agreed at once. The FMC waived their rule and we were married in the

15

Zomba Church on 28th October 1940.

We looked forward together in great expectation but it all turned out very different from our dreams.

Chapter 3

On Active Service

In 1940, Italy entered the war. Dr Kydd was proved wrong in his hope
that the war would not touch Africa. There was massive recruitment
to swell the ranks of the King's African Rifles. Then there came the
call for a chaplain to be with them, since so many of the troops were
Christians from our congregations in Nyasaland. I tried to avoid the
call but was at last personally invited by 121 to take up an appointment.
So, within a few months of marriage, Nan and I were packing up our
house and home, setting off for East Africa in the long haul by army
convoy to enable me to become a member of the East African Army
Chaplains Department.

My early assignment was in Nairobi, as chaplain to No 1 General
Hospital. It was a very large base hospital, with a predominantly
South African medical staff. I stayed in the mess, while Nan was
received most graciously and warmly at the Church of Scotland
Kikuyu Mission. She did not stay there long, however, as her training
as a company secretary soon found an outlet in the office of the
Chaplain General, Dr Yelverton. Nan's friendly and efficient way
soon made its mark and while I went off to Abyssinia, Nan served the
work of all the chaplains from the central office in Nairobi. She did
this for four years.

Soon I was off north to Abyssinia, as chaplain to the 21st EA

Brigade. I was equipped with a 1-ton truck, with the word 'Chaplain' writ large on the main structure above the cab. I had operated for a time on a motor cycle and paid visits to camps in the wide area around Nairobi and enjoyed the freedom and the speed. One day, however, a phone call came from the General, East Africa Command to the Chaplain General. He said he had often passed me on the road and while he appreciated that I was getting on with the job, he did not consider it fitting for a chaplain to be seen dashing about on a motor cycle. So I took over the truck from a South African chaplain, who was returning south. It was ideal for all the loads I wanted to carry.

In some ways I combined the duties of chaplain and welfare officer. I had a folding reading desk for use at services and carried two large boxes of books, mainly the Scriptures, in a variety of languages. I was ministering to those whose native language was English, Afrikaans, Swahili, Kikuyu, Chinyanja and two West African languages. I also carried a selection of religious books, for lending out as I travelled from unit to unit. A large space in the truck was taken up by a power generator to serve the 16-mm silent projector that I had acquired. I was most fortunate in having a good friend, Sandy Dewar, of House and McGeorge, Chemists in Nairobi. He gave me the free run of all their stock of Charlie Chaplin films. I always carried a few with me and was received with joy and expectation because of them.

Also in the truck was my tent, so handy to be set up anywhere in a camp to serve as sleeping quarters, office, study etc.

I did not travel alone. I had a marvellous staff. There was Anderson, my army driver from Northern Rhodesia. We shared the driving. He was an excellent mechanic and freely helped with other jobs that came along. Laison, my batman, had come with me from Nyasaland, where he had been houseboy in Zomba. From the time it was known that I was going to the army he pestered me to take him with me. It was the wise decision that I made. He was priceless. He was faithful in all duties and never grumbled. He and Anderson set up the film

18

show and tent as required. Laison did my cooking when I was not staying in an army mess. He attended to my clothes and helped with the selling of the books. Most important of all, this lad who had so very little formal education, proved himself quite brilliant as a translator. I had enough Chinyanja to get by with, but I soon discovered that I would have to add Swahili. I am not a fast learner of languages, so I was amazed that in two weeks after we went north from Nairobi, Laison was translating for me from Chinyanja into Swahili. They listened intently as he put my message across in his own inimitable way.

Early on, I found it necessary to turn my hand to the production of a Service Book in Chinyanja. Thousands of these were printed. The title was Tilemekeze Mulungu (Let us worship God). It was designed to allow meaningful public worship and private devotions to be maintained in all units. This was specially important since visits from chaplains were not all that frequent and the book greatly strengthened the work of those who acted as voluntary leaders of worship and pastoral care in the various units. It included full orders of service, individual prayers on a variety of private and public issues, suggested a lectionary of Bible readings and included a goodly selection of hymns.

We had our Brigade HQ at Marsabit in North Kenya and I sallied out from there, on my own, to visit other parts of the Brigade and other units along the way. I had choice moments. One day, as I headed north from Marsabit, I saw ahead of me that both sides of the road were lined by elephants, coming towards me. I had a decision to make. Did I carry on and drive between the two advancing lines, or did I halt and wait for them all to pass me by, peacefully I hoped, on either side? I decided I would feel happier in movement, so I made my way between them, a guard of honour, as it were, on each side of me. As we emerged from the encounter, I glanced at Anderson. If an African could be pale, he looked absolutely bloodless!

North Horr was the site of this isolated company of the KAR and I used to spend several happy days with them at a time. They seemed to welcome my coming but whether it was the joyous nature of our worship or the antics of Charlie Chaplin on the screen, I did not pause to enquire. North Horr was quite a distance out in desolate country. You got there just by following the tracks of those who had gone before you.

In all these Nyasa battalions, you had a sprinkling of officers and NCOs from Nyasaland and it was interesting to note the special place they held in the esteem of the African soldiers. It made one realise the multi-racial nature of the society we had created in the country, a relationship and sense of belonging together which, alas, was to be so set at risk in later days.

During 1941 and 1942, I found myself greatly involved, wherever I travelled, in conducting lectures and question-and-answer sessions on issues that were important to the troops. I covered various aspects of world affairs, trying to relate to the particular conflict in which they were involved. Most of these sessions were conducted with the African soldiers but it was most revealing to carry through the same kind of exercise with British officers or British ranks and make comparisons. The British, of course, already had a fair understanding of the issues at stake and the nature of human responsibility. Nevertheless, we worked up a fair amount of controversy over the issues of war and peace and cast our minds forward to ask, 'How can we ensure that this kind of conflict never happens again?' That tended to focus on the nature of power and authority and shared representation in various forms of government. In the African discussions, that was when we were challenged by ambitions for freedom and self-government and how to achieve adequate means of self-determination. We had to review the relationships established through the years. I could see emerging a growing demand for a change in the Protectorate or Colony status, a form of government that would match their aspirations.

There were those who questioned my right or wisdom to allow such questions and discussion. But I sensed a new area of exchange of ideas, a new hope and determination for the future that we dared not deny. Openness was of the essence.

But my supreme task, of course, remained the upbuilding of faith and of the Church. We instructed and baptised. I rejoiced in those who came to faith during their days on active service, being careful not to use my position and rank to make demands of them that would deny their right of individual choice. Yet I would not miss the chance of challenging them to a higher obedience than that represented by the army and a more far-reaching and satisfying fellowship of love beyond all that bound them together on active service.

At the end of 1941, Nan and I went off on holiday, a marvellous experience of sailing around Lake Victoria. Conditions were ideal. We were relaxed and deeply satisfied till the last night on board. It was then that there broke in upon us the news of Pearl Harbor, the callous application of force and destruction by the Japanese and the opening up of a new prospect of war escalating across the world.

It transformed the situation in East Africa from being a completed war zone to being once again in the front line, as troops were required for action in the Far East. Recruitment was stepped up and as 1942 developed, I was sent south to Nyasaland and Northern Rhodesia to recruit chaplains to serve the expanding army.

Nan and I travelled in the 1-ton truck, all the way through Tanzania, through Northern Nyasaland to Blantyre and Zomba. I addressed the church courts and made my appeal. The result was more than adequate. Two European chaplains were ready to join and six African ministers volunteered. I had them signed up and returned north to prepare for their training and posting. My own position changed. I was no longer on my own, but as the senior non-Anglican, non-Roman chaplain I was promoted to be Senior Chaplain to the Forces (3rd Class) with a wide coverage of chaplaincy services to plan and administer.

The new chaplains arrived and we had a training centre established at which I shared responsibility with a young and rather extreme Anglo-Catholic padre from Tanzania. He got off to a very bad start by suggesting to my African colleagues that they were not really ordained at all, in the light of his understanding of Church orders and authority. I had the matter sorted out at the highest level and he had to acknowledge a completely new world of church relationship and brotherly respect. That initial clearing of the ground worked wonders for the spirit and life of the Chaplains Department. We had several marvellous training conferences of all serving chaplains together with the Honorary Chaplains to the Forces who were appointed throughout Kenya.

There grew up a new concept of the reality and unity of the Church, which was to have its repercussions throughout the territories once the war was over.

My new found rank meant that I was called upon to deal with problems arising from other chaplains' work. I received a message from a brigadier to call and see him. It meant a long haul for me but I went. The Brigadier was a Scot, of very distinguished service and a staunch member of the Kirk. His demand was immediate. He wanted his chaplain reposted out of his sight and out of his units. I knew something of the said European chaplain's eccentricities and tried to move round the subject of his particular habits and actions, but all to no avail. The crux of the matter was this: 'We cannot any longer tolerate his over-cheerful appearance in the mess every morning, when some of us are feeling under the weather, only to hear him call out "Are we all HAPPY". He must be moved.'

I extricated myself from the situation as best I could to turn with fresh enthusiasm to giving guidance and support to the African chaplains. What a joy they were to me! – Clement and Samuel, Augustine and Yona, David and Charles. They grew in the experience of their new-found responsibilities. I saw them become more evangelical and knowledgeable of their charges than ever they had been in their village setting. I rejoiced that one of them became more deeply committed to upholding standards of behaviour than ever he had been before. It was moving to travel around with them and share with them thoughts on their ministry and prayer for their work. My planning for them brought up again the issue of motor cycles. Thrilled though I was personally to the delight and freedom of the motor cycle, I just could not bear the thought of committing my chaplains to life on 750cc Harley Davidsons, which was what the army offered. They were powerful machines and I represented to Command HQ that I could not risk the lives of my chaplains upon them. Other, satisfactory, arrangements were made.

One of the great joys of these war years was the close links that Nan and I established with the Church in Kenya and in particular with the staff at Kikuyu, Tumutumu and Chogoria. Kikuyu was an early port of call when we first came up from Nyasaland. The Calderwoods, Marjorie and George were kindness itself. On frequent return visits

Heading for Burao, Somaliland.

23

we got to know the Patersons (Education) and Dr Andrew Shaw at the hospital. We had happy times with Helen Ramsay and Margaret Burt. Nearby was the Alliance High School, so we were in touch with one area of secondary education. Also nearby was a large army Signals camp, so it got regular chaplaincy attention! This signals unit was special, as it was staffed with West African troops. I conducted the services in English but carried Scriptures in their West African languages to sell to them.

When I set out on lines of communication to the north and Abyssinia, I always stopped off at Tumutumu. I stayed with Dr Monteith Brown and his wife and family. They were always so welcoming. I soon knew all the activities of the station and even took part in operations at the hospital.

Chogoria was more off the road towards Mount Kenya, but we reached it on holidays, enjoying the hospitality of the famous Dr Clive Irvine and his wife and the friendly greetings of Peggy Ferguson, the nursing sister. We were greatly impressed with the singing in the church, in which the drums played an important role. The volume of singing was tremendous.

After my promotion, my office was at Southern Area HQ, outside Nairobi. Nan and I stayed at the Devon Hotel, though I was more often than not, on tour over a wide area that took in Abyssinia, Somaliland and Tanganyika. I also had a long haul up to Southern Sudan. It was on that journey that I had the only accident through all my army service. A tyre burst and the truck turned over. There was surprisingly little damage, even with the generator hitting the roof. There was a fearful moment when I dashed round to the back of the truck and could see no sign of Laison, who always rode in the back. I was afraid that he was somewhere under all the tumbled contents, but, wise man, he had jumped out as the truck began skidding and now walked up to rejoin us with a broad grin on his face.

Every Sunday, Nan attended St Andrews Church, helped with the

Sunday School and was thoroughly at home in the manse, with the Howiesons. Once in a while I managed to attend and preached on occasions. When Robert Howieson had a spell of illness, the Army permitted me to take charge of St Andrews for a month. I greatly enjoyed the experience. St Andrews had a great variety of activity, for social and spiritual purposes. Scottish country dancing was a special feature and the Sunday School facilities were greatly appreciated. The congregation, of a Sunday, was a marvellous mixture of civilians and service personnel. As the main non-Anglican church, those attending came from a great variety of church backgrounds and welded together powerfully in worship and service.

Alas, my latter days in the Army were clouded by sorrow and conflict.

Nan was about to have a baby and we were absolutely delighted, and eagerly looking forward. She stayed at Kikuyu and was well looked after, even spoiled. The days drew on. The babe was born but lived only a few hours. We buried him, named Andrew Beveridge, at Kikuyu. We were surrounded by much caring and concern. Nan was very depressed at first, but to my great joy, soon broke through and became her lively positive self again. How very timely it was, because I was facing a battle that I sensed I could not win. Nan's knowledge of the Chaplain's Department stood me in good stead and her whole-hearted support for the stand I was taking was a constant delight to me.

I have emphasised quite a bit, the right of the individual to make choices, especially where faith and witness are involved. I often felt the impact of this voluntary offering of oneself when conducting worship, in the open air, in a camp in the early morning or as the shades of evening gathered. As you looked out on a congregation such as St Andrews, it was wonderful to sense the spontaneity and joy of sharing and expressing one's faith. There was one occasion in my experience as Senior Chaplain, when I found this spontaneity entirely absent.

For some time we had been under a new Deputy Assistant Chaplain General, who replaced the beloved Eric Yelverton. This new man was set on stepping up the participation in public worship, as he embarked on an intensive campaign of parade services throughout the Command and especially in Nairobi.

I soon sensed the difference.

True, the attendance grew but the whole atmosphere changed. There was a resentment even among those who had chosen to attend before. I heard from units of the blasphemous utterances of many as they were prepared for parade to go to church and raised the issue in the Chaplain's Department but got little or no support. Taking advice in a variety of quarters, I decided I would have to act myself. One of those consulted was Bertie Baird. He was a pathologist of distinction, serving in the army, a son of the manse in Broomhill Church in Glasgow, where his father had preceded Turner Kennedy. I had performed his wedding in St Andrews Church, Nairobi. From the outset he was all the way with me in my objections. He encouraged me to take the issue to the top and refuse to budge. I intimated to the DACG that I was not prepared to conduct services, attended under duress and with no sense of personal anticipation. I was called before the General, East Africa Command. He was sympathetic to my point of view but made it clear he could not go against a provision of King's Regulations.

The DACG tried another tack to win me over. He produced an unexpected argument that I was depriving myself of the just and due honours that were coming to me. He divulged that my name was on the list for the honour of OBE, but that if I continued on my present campaign, the honour would certainly be forfeit. I was not impressed. Events were moving fast in the ending of the war in Europe and I found myself asking, 'Was this perhaps the time to move out and prepare for a post-war ministry?' I was conscious of the responsibility

I had to the African chaplains I had recruited and supported. However, they were now well established and I had their whole-hearted support in the stand I was taking. I took the plunge. I offered my resignation from the army and applied for travel facilities to proceed to the UK. The resignation was accepted, though not, I think, without regret. To my surprise, the resignation was not to take effect till I was back in the UK.

Nan and I were granted special travel arrangements. We set off in early May 1945 by what used to be the millionaire's route, along the Nile to Cairo. There were fifteen changes on the way, using rail, road and steamer transport. It took us two weeks. On the steamer to Khartoum, we celebrated VE Day, the end of the war in Europe. After a short stay in Cairo, where we made the most of sightseeing opportunities, we embarked upon a troopship at Alexandria, bound for the UK and to our delight and surprise found ourselves sailing up the Clyde to disembark at Glasgow.

Looking back I realised what an incredible experience we had had in Africa, myself for six years and Nan for five.

I was demobbed at York and picked up my blue demob suit, which didn't really fit me well, so, later I passed it on to an African colleague.

I immediately reverted to being on the staff of the Foreign Mission Committee, received a warm welcome with immediate talk of our return to Nyasaland the following year. At home, I found plenty to do, undertaking many speaking engagements, enjoying reporting on the impact of the war on the Church, myself and the African. I wrote articles that were not only descriptive but aimed to be prophetic. I raised the challenge to provide outlets for the new dreams and expectations of the Africans in post-war conditions. I underlined the questions they had asked, the new sense of identity they possessed and the impatience with which they looked forward to sharing in the re-creating of their life, their land and the government of their country.

Chapter 4

The Aftermath of War

I had no doubt about returning to Nyasaland. I was keen to engage upon the follow up to my war experience and to make contact with the men I had known in uniform as they returned to take up civilian life.

We returned to Zomba, to the job I had done before the call-up in 1941 and to some extra jobs that had not been foreseen. It had always been the practice since away back in the days of Dr Hetherwick that there was a seat on the Legislative Council for a missionary member. This started in 1908, and through the years, Dr Hetherwick, Dr Laws, James Reid, Duncan Mackenzie, W.P. Young, J.F. Alexander had in turn served so far as the Church of Scotland was concerned. Each had made his own contribution to fulfil what was designed to be 'an independent representation of the native community'. A recent publication on Scottish missionaries as legislators notes

> During the intervening half-century (1908-1958), a total of thirteen European clergymen, who had come to Nyasaland to propagate the Gospel, were called upon to act as spokesmen for the Africans in the law-making process. Much can be learned about the attitudes and behaviour of these Scottish missionary-legislators from Kirk and Government records that are now

available. Their performance in representing a constituency which lacked the power to hold them responsible, provided a dramatic expression of paternalism and trusteeship in a changing Colonial situation.

On my return from war service, I was invited to take up this appointment and agreed to do so, believing that it would tie in well with my concerns for the Africans' interests post war.

So we established our home and renewed our contacts throughout the wide area of Zomba and Domasi districts. Week by week we visited village churches and preached in Zomba. Next door to us was Mary Lowe, in charge of district educational work with special reference to women teachers. She often took Nan with her on her tours. These trips had to ease off when it was clear that Nan was about to have another child. The hospital staff at Zomba were fully supportive. No one could foresee the end of the process, though Nan did have her fears and anxieties as the months passed by. The child was born and it was broken to me that Nan was far from well and would have to stay in hospital. Erine Petrie took charge of little Anne in her own home and I often spent a night there while fulfilling my work and my daily visits to hospital. A few weeks later Nan died and I was faced with all kinds of decisions.

With the help of Anne Lord, a missionary nurse, I took little Anne home to the care of Nan's family. I seriously considered changing over to the home ministry. However, there was an inner sense of a story half told, a work far from accomplished and the strange expectation that I was just on the verge of new demands and new fulfilment, for which all the rest was just a preparation. I returned to Nyasaland in February 1948.

A visiting team from Scotland had been out to Central Africa, seeking a new plan of action for the work in Nyasaland and Northern Rhodesia on Church and Mission business. As a result, Douglas

Benzies was appointed Regional Secretary for the area. To everyone's dismay and disappointment, he died within a few weeks of taking up the appointment.

An approach to me to succeed him was declined, though I did accept an interim appointment and travelled widely through Nyasaland and Northern Rhodesia. I recall several very difficult journeys in the wet season, through flooded rivers to reach the Council meetings on time. On all these wanderings, I was accompanied by the redoubtable Laison, who had been with me before the war and all through the war. My task was to keep under review in the various areas the progress of integration of Church and Mission and to reassess the balance of our various emphases in Medical, Educational and Evangelistic work. I operated from Zomba, maintaining my ministry there and improving my contacts with Government and local African associations in both

Married; Andrew and Barbara.

territories. These were two very demanding years but the pressurised timetable, as it were, worked wonders for me.

Then came my real breakthrough. In my work, I found great pleasure in frequent visits to the Girls' School in Blantyre. Of course, my visits were part of my work but there was more to it than that. Barbara Young, the headmistress and in charge of Teaching Training, was first class at her job and impressed all who came in touch with her. She did more than that for me. I began to realise how much she attracted me and what a joy life would be shared with her. To my delight she responded to my advances and we spoke of the future with excitement and expectation. We tried to keep our romance a secret but in 1949, the news broke and we were rejoicing in the many who thought with us that this was the most marvellous happening.

Barbara went home several months ahead of the wedding to make preparations. I followed just shortly before the date fixed, the 28th of December 1950. I don't know why I hurried! Barbara arrived fifteen minutes late for the wedding ceremony!

It was a glorious occasion. There were lots of guests at the Forman Church, Leven. The ceremony was conducted by my elder brother, David, minister of Forman Church, where Barbara and her family were all members. My younger brother, George, also a minister, acted as best man. Barbara's sister, Bessie was bridesmaid, while young Russell Davies, her nephew, acted as page. It was great having so many family and friends around us. The older generation was represented by Barbara's father and by my mother. The friends brought together a marvellous cross-section of those who had shared with us at College, through our training, or in subsequent mission service. Of course, the farming community was well represented. The young farmers decided to have some fun. They hoisted me up on top of the taxi as we were about to leave. They took off my shoes and then my socks. To their great surprise and delight, they discovered I was wearing two pairs of socks, to cope with the cold.

We had our honeymoon in Edinburgh, facing a long wait at the ferry and enduring agonies a few days later as our new car disappeared from George Street. We had been shopping and left our purchases in the car, while we did some more acquiring of goods and returned to find the car gone. An identical model was just next to where ours had been. We went down to the police post at the Mound and reported the loss. A policeman came back with us and we felt very conspicuous. When we got back to the police box, there was a phone call from someone who was very embarrassed. His wife had left their car in George Street for her husband to pick up. When he arrived home, she asked him, what on earth he had been buying – meaning all our parcels. Then they discovered it was not their car. We soon sorted it out but what a coincidence that two Morris cars should have been set next to each other and that the keys of the two should have been interchangeable.

Before I left Nyasaland, I had handed over the Regional Secretaryship to Neil Bernard and Barbara and I embarked upon a most interesting and shared period of deputation work throughout Scotland.

We returned to the manse in Zomba in 1951. I was again District Missionary, Secretary of Mission Council and resumed my place as missionary member of Legislative Council. While I moved freely and positively in Church affairs, I found I was having to devote more and more time and attention to those subjects related to power and authority in Government, feeding in as it did to my membership of the Legislative Council. There was increasing talk of a Federation of States – Southern Rhodesia, Northern Rhodesia and Nyasaland. I listened to the talk, studied the arguments, tried to put it all in a historic setting, not only in relation to the past but in consideration of the future. This was particularly related to the African, for whom I had developed such a high regard in terms of his abilities, his potential and his hopes.

I had no hesitation in weighing in on the Anti-Federation side and made my speeches in Legislative Council to that effect. My contacts built up with African political leaders, not all of whom appreciated my representing African interests but increasingly expressed delight, amazement and support for the stand I was taking.

I was aware that my role as a missionary member of Legislative Council was changing radically. I was presuming to reflect African needs as I saw them, to interpret African hopes as I understood them and to argue for an honest development of the historical purpose and promise since 1891. But seldom, if ever before, had the missionary representative so distanced himself from the official and unofficial element in Legislative Council, as I found myself doing.

At one stage, I felt I was gaining support from some of the unofficials, whose concern for the freedom and development of Nyasaland, like my own, left no place for the overtones of political domination from the south and economic bondage to a predominantly European vision. But increasingly, the unofficial community were won over by a feeling that London was opting out of this part of Africa and was only too keen to pass its responsibility, both politically and economically to the developing unification of the two Rhodesias and Nyasaland.

I must pay tribute to the freedom that was always assured to me in relation to the officials. Many of them were as opposed to Federation as I was. The Governor, Sir Geoffrey Colby, shared my convictions in a very real sense and at one point, there was a distinct possibility that he would resign rather than be at the head of a Government that imposed Federation against the expressed will of the African people.

But Federation was imposed. I had plenty to do in the Church and could have turned away from the political sphere to fulfil my hopes and expectations of a growing and increasingly meaningful church structure and life. But there came an invitation to occupy the post under the Federal Constitution that allowed for a Nominated European Representative of African Interests. At first, I recoiled. Would not my acceptance be seen as a denial, betrayal, surrender of all I had been saying and standing for over the years. How would the African in the Church and in the wider Nyasaland fellowship interpret my action?

So I turned it down.

There followed a period of anxiety and inner conflict. African opinion came to me loud and clear, saying, 'We'd rather see someone in the post whom we can trust to interpret what happens in the light of our hopes and fears and future rather than a Yes-man for the Federation, aiming to get a view across whatever we might think.'

Chapter 5

Federal Assembly

Having thought it through, I accepted the appointment. It was probably the hardest decision of my life. I was under no illusions. A friend said, 'You'll be massacred from both sides.' I asked myself: How balanced could I remain in my judgements and presentation of the situation as I saw it developing. I was suspect in some European quarters, with the old story – 'Let the Church stick to the Gospel and keep out of politics'. I must, therefore, be sure at every turn in my own mind that the issues on which I spoke, were capable of a decision in terms of inter-racial justice and compassion for the underprivileged. I must hold fast to the matter that had been uppermost in my mind since the beginning of the Federal controversy. How does this or that decision affect the long standing commitment of the British Government to be a Protecting power in the interests of African development and fulfilment?

In those early days I was greatly helped by the attitude of officials, especially the Governor. He forestalled me in one of the demands I was about to make, by underlining his conviction that the fact that I was nominated by him must not limit my freedom of expression on any line of argument I felt compelled to take in the Federal Assembly. That matched exactly my own concern. Geoffrey Colby and I had many heart to heart talks during the period he was Governor and never once did he seek to influence my method of presentation or argument. Indeed he was often outspoken enough in the privacy of his office in agreeing with the line I was taking. I always got the strong impression that he disagreed fundamentally with the imposition of Federation and lost ground himself with Whitehall in taking that line.

I was happy in the association I built up with many members of the Federal Assembly from the three territories. My early concern was with the likely unanimity of view of the African Affairs Board, the watchdog committee charged with examining all planned legislation and practical action that might be detrimental to the interests of the African. There were three members from each territory on the Board – the European Nominated members and the two African members from each territory.

I had a happy relationship with my African colleagues from Nyasaland, W. Manyowa Chirwa and Clement Kumbikano. Clement I had known for many years but Manyowa was a new friend. We made a good team, quickly establishing agreement in our line of procedure. We toured Nyasaland together, addressing large meetings and small groups on the matters that came before the Federal Assembly, finding the interest we expected and facing many challenging questions. We stressed the dangers we saw in the Federal structure as it developed. They were good enough to say we were doing a good job, though of course, we met those who felt we had no right to be there at all. Our meetings did not pass unnoticed by the authorities. What we said was carefully monitored and passed on but no one tried to restrict our movements or our presentations.

With the other members of the African Affairs Board, we formed a key element in the Federal set-up, The African Affairs Board settled down well once we got to know each other. The two Africans from Northern Rhodesia were very close to us and in ready agreement on most issues. It took longer to find any rapport with the two Africans from Southern Rhodesia. They came from a very different background.

This was a new experience for them to be in any representative capacity. They took longer to shake free from the order of things they knew in their country and be fully critical.

The two other European representatives for African interests were the Rev Percy Ibbotson from Southern Rhodesia and Dr Haslam from Northern Rhodesia. Ibbotson was a Methodist minister but I never got close to him. He was enthusiastic about the Federation, strongly supportive of the Southern Rhodesian way of life and very suspicious of our emphasis from the north. Haslam, as a retired government doctor, was altogether different – gracious and co-operative. He was succeeded, after a time, by Sir John Moffat, of the famous missionary family. With Sir John, I at once formed a close and warm association. We saw eye to eye on many matters, so that our speeches were in a real sense complementary and so it continued till the end of my parliamentary career.

I had entered into the political scene with a clear hope and expectation that I might act as a communicator between black and white, seeking to be fair to each and to find a way forward in partnership. There were those who doubted this possibility from the beginning. As time went on, I had to adjust my presentation. I discovered that the Southern Rhodesian Press headlined those parts of my speeches that sought to be understanding of the European position but ignored the submission I made for priority for African needs and advancement and against discrimination in its many forms. I had no alternative. I dropped my attempt to be, in all things, the friend of both sides and concentrated on my prime responsibility of speaking for the Africans. I must not give the impression that the Press ignored me. One newspaper wrote that Doig 'brings the murmur of the Covenanters with him – a typical member of the Scottish Church, fired with missionary zeal, eternally conscious of the traditions which his church holds in Nyasaland' (*The Citizen*).

Through it all, I maintained a close contact with my home base in

Edinburgh. In 1953, when I was asked to serve on the Federal Assembly, the Foreign Mission Committee refused to grant permission. They reluctantly insisted that the staffing situation was such that I could not be spared for such an appointment. They conceded my contention that it could be advantageous to test from within the Legislature the claims of those who maintained that such a Union could benefit the Africans. There had been some hard argument at 121 summed up in the Convener's statement: 'Are we to risk still worse relationships with the Nyasaland Government and open ourselves to the charge that we are not prepared to sacrifice immediate mission interests for the sake of the long term African interests – or are we to risk doing great damage to our own proper mission and church work?'

The Committee chose the first risk and was not altogether displeased when I disobeyed instructions and in effect, forced acceptance of the second risk. They declined to ask for my resignation and agreed to

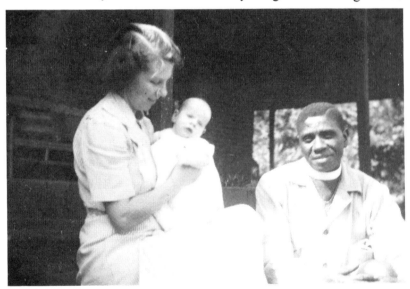

Frederick Chintali at Peter's baptism.

second me to the Federal Assembly for two years. I maintained close links with the pastoral and preaching work of the Church of Central Africa, Presbyterian both in Nyasaland and in Southern Rhodesia during sessions of the Federal Assembly. In 1955, I requested that my secondment be extended until 1958 and this request was readily granted.

Life was not easy for us as a family during these Federal days. I owe so much to Barbara for her constant support and understanding in all the decisions I had to make. Peter was just one year old when I made the decision, and we had to move out of our house in Zomba and accept accommodation provided by the Government at Domasi. It was a good house with congenial neighbours (Tommy Thomson, Government Development Officer, Mary Kennedy and Etta Smith, District Health workers and also the Teacher Training staff nearby). It was in my old mission district and we were at home in all church activities and contacts. We had to battle against a certain criticism from some members of the mission staff and Barbara especially had to bear the weight of estrangement. Most of the staff were loyal and supportive to us all the way through.

The family was a constant joy to us. Peter was born on 11th November 1952 and soon established himself as a boy with a will of his own. He made friends with all the Africans and kept an eye on me when I was out and about, organising the Church. He was fond of climbing trees and I remember, leading discussion in a group under the spreading branches of a large tree while from a short distance away, Peter kept an eye on me from the upper branches of another tree.

He loved toy cars and engines and built up a wonderful collection. The only trouble was that he loved burying them in the ground, so that they were safe from those who might have wanted to take them. I shudder to think how many toys must lie still buried in the grounds of the Blantyre Mission.

Isabelle arrived on 17th March 1955. She was born in Zomba hospital. The Parliament was in session, so I had to go to Salisbury and wait for news from home. I remember well how, during a debate in Parliament, the Parliamentary Officer came down the passageway bearing a note for me. I was conscious of all eyes being upon me, for they knew what I was expecting. I gave a sign that all was well and there was a murmur of congratulation and applause. So you could say that Isabelle by her birth, made a very special impact on the proceedings.

Isabelle was a very lively wee girl, making herself useful to all around and increasing their joy. She appeared on several occasions looking radiant as a bridesmaid at weddings both black and white.

We had some great holiday experiences. We made a long trek to the north of Nyasaland, renewing friendships and deepening our understanding of the people and how they felt. That was the trip on which Peter decided to cut Isabelle's hair. I don't think his efforts were appreciated but Isabelle took it all in her stride.

One of our special holidays was when we took Meta Douglas (Treasurer at the Mission) with us by car to Southern Rhodesia to enjoy life in the Wankie Game Park. The children loved the animals and Peter and Isabelle played with the small monkeys who kept climbing all over the car. We went on to the Victoria Falls, lost in admiration of the mighty flow of water and happy to be appreciating what once moved Livingstone so deeply in his days.

There was variety in our lives with those periods that we spent in Salisbury for the meetings of the Federal Assembly and then the long tours that I made throughout Nyasaland. Our visits to Salisbury gave us a chance to assess the trend of thought among the Europeans of Southern Rhodesia. Especially in the city, Salisbury, we were conscious of a very different attitude to Africans. We stayed in Meikle's Hotel on more than one occasion. I have never forgotten the greeting we got one day from the woman who cleaned the room. She said to Barbara,

'One of these blacks came looking for your husband. I told him to get back to the gutter where he belonged.' Poor woman! She could not believe that he was highly educated, able to hold down a job she could never have looked at, and a powerful figure in his own society.

Then there was that day when Barbara Castle, Labour MP from London came fact finding in the Federation. I arranged some of her programme, and entertained her at the hotel. It seemed a good idea to invite to dinner with her my colleagues, Manyowa Chirwa and Clement Kumbikano. You should have seen the face of the manager, when I turned up with my guests, requesting to be shown to the table I had spoken for. He just could not believe his eyes – Africans to be provided for in his hotel! He said something about, how could I do this to him, asked us to wait in a secluded part of the corridor and then showed us to a table, behind a pillar, concealed by many pot plants, where we were unseeing and unseen. We laughed about it, felt we had scored a victory and enjoyed our dinner.

My relationship with white colleagues in the Assembly was quite easy. They showed me the parliamentary courtesies, but in varying degrees, showed they disapproved of my presence and of the function I had taken upon myself.

Several individuals stand out in my recollection. There was Godfrey Huggins, later Lord Malvern, the first Prime Minister of the Federation. He was an impressive character and a natural leader. His medical training developed an essential caring quality for individuals. Alas! He could not use it to cross the racial barriers. He was powerful in debate, could be scathing in his judgements and never disguised the fact that he did not want a Federation of this sort. He was uncomfortable, when reminded of the historic emphasis from the north in the promise of Protectorates leading to self-determination. He would obviously have preferred to have self-governing status conferred on Southern Rhodesia by itself. He was not always a good listener, when points of view expressed were not to his liking. He used his hearing aid to great effect, ostentatiously removing it from his ear and placing it on the desk in front of him. I used to feel I was really getting under his skin, when he acted in this way, when I was speaking.

He was succeeded by Roy Welensky, a large cheerful man from Northern Rhodesia. He was of humble origins, was well read and most knowledgeable about public affairs. He had spent his days in the railway service and kept himself on easy friendly terms with all with whom he had worked. At Government receptions, we used to hear those he had invited to be present, marvelling and rejoicing that he never forgot his old mates. I had no difficulty whatsoever in maintaining meaningful contact with Roy Welensky.

He expressed agreement with many of my arguments and claimed to share much of my vision. But he believed I was rushing things. 'These things must come,' he would say, 'but not yet, not in our lifetime.' It would take many years, he claimed, to advance the Africans to be ready for partnership, to have the gifts to merit equality with whites.

Knowing the mounting expectation and hope among the Africans of Nyasaland and appreciating their potential, I just had to answer, 'You haven't got that kind of time.' Deep down, I believe, he accepted that. Publicly he dared not admit it.

Macintyre, Minister of Finance, was one who had come up the hard way of self-discovery and self-advancement. He was most able and commanded respect wherever he went. I always felt that he was content to restrict himself to the financial problems of the Federation and tended to fight shy of being involved in the political warfare. He was a Scot and a teetotaller. I recall how, at an official dinner in Blantyre, where drinks were laid on as part of the meal, he ordered an orangeade. To his surprise, though he didn't show it, he was charged for it and paid up with a smile.

Ian Smith was a very tough character with an impressive record. A skilled and highly successful fighter pilot during the war, he always seemed to wear rather a supercilious look. He was not likeable but had to be taken seriously since he represented most effectively the extreme wing of the Federal party, adhering strongly to the Southern Rhodesian concept of white supremacy. In many ways, I felt sorry for him. I had opportunities for discussion with him in private, apart from the occasions when we crossed swords in the Assembly. Of course, he recognised the existence of the African but to Smith, he was only an employee on the farm. He saw him as having a very restricted field of service and a duty to be performed to his white master. I talked to him of the African I knew – courteous, of happy disposition of growing ability, of amazing potential when given the chance to develop and accept responsibility. He just didn't recognise the character of whom I spoke. He simply didn't want to. After the Federation was unscrambled, Smith, of course, became Prime Minister of the continuing Southern Rhodesia. I followed his doings with great interest and was not in the least surprised when he declared his unilateral act of independence. It did not last long and Britain had the satisfaction of playing a notable part in the creation of a sovereign state, Zimbabwe under the accepted leadership of Mugabe.

As the years passed, I could sense a move towards change. Southern Rhodesia was not content with the Federal Constitution. One began to hear comments aspiring to Dominion status. But even more alarming was the indication that the British Government was considering likely changes to the Federal Constitution. Malvern had talks with the British Government. The growth of a Dominion Party in Southern Rhodesia with a strong emphasis on Dominion status and increased control of internal affairs made Welensky tell me that he could see them winning the next election. Cullinan, the party whip says (Hansard p. 1389) 'I do believe the ball has started rolling now, the preliminary stage of obtaining Dominion status and that next year, we can go further.' There were those who saw this as purely related to external affairs, but it was clear that this was but the first move to more effective internal control, combined as it was with a vicious attack on the Colonial Office. All the faults of the Northern Territories were seen to stem from the Colonial Office and its policy. There was constant reiteration of how much better they controlled their natives in Southern Rhodesia. The Africans in the north were bewildered by this attack but even more by the failure of the Colonial Office to answer and fight back.

I sensed a growing demand among the whites in Southern Rhodesia for radical change. They felt the United Kingdom Government would have to be challenged to what extent they still believed in Protectorate status for the Northern Territories. Also, I sensed a growing demand among the Africans of Nyasaland to step up their opposition to Federation and to call for a decisive action to remove their fears. In 1957, I carried out a three-week tour in the north of the country, visiting Edingeni, Loudon, Mzimba, Ekwendeni, Mzuzu, Nkata Bay, Rumpi, Chikurumaembe, Katumbi, Livingstonia, Deep Bay and Karonga. Everywhere I had a warm welcome, was deeply impressed by their grasp of affairs and their reasoning against some of the more hopeful points I made about Federation. Most of all I gained a feeling of deep disquiet in growing opinion and plan for action.

It was sheer nonsense of Lennox Boyd to give suave answers in the House of Commons as if all were well and of how the Federal leaders were fully aware of the need for African support and confidence (2 May). The Federal leaders either didn't know or didn't care, but my considered opinion after this tour in the north was that African feeling about Federation was more bitter now than at any time in the past. It was not just Federal leaders that were now coming in for criticism but the intentions of the British Government were being very much called in question. Moreover, the representatives for African interests from Nyasaland (Chirwa, Kumbikano and myself) were now being accused of staying in the Assembly only for what we could make out of it financially. The sum total of the verdict from the meetings was 'African representatives must come out now. Only when the seats are vacant will Britain listen to our objections and realise we mean what we say.'

I had a long talk with Lennox Boyd but was gravely disappointed when he made his statements later. He came using the same phrases that have been the cry of Southern Rhodesian leaders for so long – that Federation is here to stay and that the Government must be in the hands of civilised and responsible persons. As to the first, he gave no indication as to what the British Government would contend for within an enduring Federation and for the second, he ought to have known that these words, especially 'civilised' have been so debased here as to be useless.

The Prime Minister of the Federation returned from London insisting that the British Government would look favourably upon a new status for the Federation in 1960. He did not try to conceal his belief that Independence is assured for 1960 or as a result of the conference then.

My deep disquiet was only increased when the Franchise Bill was produced. It was totally opposed by two-thirds of the African Affairs Board as detrimental to African Interests. Yet it was approved by the British Government. I made a special journey to Britain to lobby Government ministers and members. I addressed meetings throughout Britain but all to no avail.

I had a most valuable session in Edinburgh with Dr Hastings Banda. We reviewed the situation, firmly agreeing that the Federation must not be allowed to continue a day longer than possible. We concentrated on fixing dates: when should I resign from the Federal Assembly, with effective publicity of the reasons for my decision? When should Dr Banda return to lead the Independence struggle that must surely be promoted in Nyasaland?

On 23rd June 1958, I resigned my seat, giving reasons in my letter to the Speaker, which, however, were not read out to the Assembly.

The letter read:

> I beg to inform you that I have decided to resign my seat in the Federal Assembly as from midnight, 23rd June 1958. I have also communicated my decision to the Governor of Nyasaland.
>
> My conviction that I can no longer usefully represent African Interests in the Federal Assembly rests upon two facts.
>
> 1. The setting aside of the reservation of the African Affairs Board in regard to the Constitution Amendment and Franchise Bills has so weakened the position of the Board as to render it quite ineffective as a safeguard for African Interests. It is true that the Board has no power of veto but it is equally true that the members of the Board consider all the aspects of a Bill and decide if on balance it is disadvantageous. That this was the opinion of two-thirds of the Board and of all the members representing African Interests from the two Northern Territories, both European and African should have given the Federal Government and even more the British Government furiously to think before pressing on regardless of the consequences for the Board. In my opinion, further service on the Board is useless.
>
> 2. The action of the Governments in insisting upon a fundamental change to the Federal Constitution (a) while African support has still not been won for Federation at all and (b) despite the implicit assurance in the wording of the Constitution that territorial practice would continue (Section 13 of the Constitution) (c) despite the increased suspicion and uneasiness of the Africans and declared opposition through statutory councils and unofficial bodies and (d) without offering any explanation or proof of the urgency of such fundamental change – altogether forms a course of action I could not possibly defend or commend to the African and I feel compelled in the interests both of

Africans and of the peace of these territories to protest further by my resignation.

I remain

Yours sincerely

(Rev) Andrew B Doig

I took good care that the reasons received due publicity and I greatly appreciated the support of the Press in this regard.

So I withdrew from my active participation in the political scene. I cannot but note how deeply touched I was by hearing that one month after I resigned, there was moved in the Federal Assembly, a record of appreciation of my services. Wellington Chirwa very skilfully put forward the motion. A number of African and European members took part, crediting me with speaking 'in a moderate way and with a dignified manner'. Dr Scott of Lusaka, like myself hailing from Carluke, referred to my covenanting background. Julian Greenfield, Minister of Law, did not disguise his opposition to me but conceded 'modesty, extreme lucidity and fearlessness in his speaking'.

Sir John Moffat was loyal as ever and summed it up by saying: 'It is unlikely that a motion such as this will ever be repeated but it is quite certain that it will never be more richly deserved.'

Reading over the debate, I felt humble – and uplifted. My ministry's most testing period was completed.

EXTRACTS FROM THE FEDERAL HANSARD

Reading over my speeches made in the Federal Assembly, I find it surprising but reassuring that despite my fully committed opposition to Federation, I did not aim to destroy it. Indeed, through the debates, I sought to challenge the members to make a success of the venture by deliberate moves to racial understanding and accepted racial equality.

1st July 1954   Uniform Public Holidays

Rev A.B. Doig: Mr Speaker, I approach this motion before the House with a great deal of sympathy with the intention behind it. It is obviously in the interests of all concerned that the basic public holidays should be the same in the three territories and I can see no difficulty at all in producing a Bill that would define certain basic public holidays that would be acceptable to all. However, I think recognition has to be given to the different background and tradition of the territories composing the Federation.

Mention has been made of Rhodes and Founders Days celebrated in the Rhodesias and it is only natural by the history of these two territories, that such days should be observed. It is no dishonour to Rhodes or his memory if the third territory of the Federation should not feel so deeply on the matter or his commemoration. I do not expect a Sassenach or the Irish to be as enthusiastic about St Andrew's Day as I am and there are backgrounds to Nyasaland's history that have to be borne in mind if we are to give due place to the total heritage that is being brought into the Federation.

The vexed question has arisen of a Federation Day and I must give a considerable measure of support to the Honourable African members from the Northern Territories in their estimate of the reaction of their people to such a day being proclaimed a public holiday The suggestion that there should be a Federation Day comes as no surprise to any of us but I would feel personally that in the immediate case it would be better that Federation Day be proclaimed if it is necessary as a day, without making it a public holiday. To proclaim a public holiday, is not just to hope that somehow things will be organised. On the African side and with the District Administration assisting, it involves a considerable amount of planning and willing co-operation of all concerned. Such a public holiday as the Queen's Birthday, in the Northern Territories is made an occasion when the community and schools in particular seek to express what this means to their land, and to take part in it by games and plays, to make it known to the public generally and to rejoice in it. When the day comes that we have drawn together, and are found appreciating one another, evolving true partnership, that will be the time to think of a public holiday called Federation Day but not before. If such a day were declared a public holiday in the immediate future, I can foresee grave danger of it being a day of considerable difficulty for arrangements by District Commissioners and others, a day of tension and misunderstanding within the African community itself and that surely is something we do not wish to see. So I plead that if the Government is called upon to introduce such a bill, it will bear in mind the need to recognise the different backgrounds and traditions of the territories concerned and in particular, on this question of Federation Day, I would suggest that it be not included at the moment in the list of public holidays.

29th July 1954   Equality of treatment of all races

Mr Speaker: When the debate was adjourned on 20th July, the question was a motion by Mr Yamba: That equal treatment be accorded immediately to all races in all public places within the Federation and that such action be enforced by legislation to be passed by the Federal Assembly.

Rev A.B. Doig: In the debate on this subject, very great stress was laid on the unsuitability of the terms of the motion from the legislative and practical points of view. It was stressed that some of the things that could be assumed as being asked for were in fact not within the legislative competence of this House and no doubt some are already prepared to rule out the motion purely on that ground. Such an action would be entirely legitimate, but I venture to suggest with all respect, rather unwise.

How often are we constrained in life to admit that actions that may be unquestionably lawful are equally strikingly inexpedient. To dismiss this motion because of its inexact or unsatisfactory wording would to my mind be a classic example of this inexpedience.

To my mind there is a far greater issue here. What is the prevailing spirit that has been evidenced here? Have we taken a step forward in fostering interracial understanding and sympathy? Have we by what we say here erected any new signposts to show where we are going in this multi-racial society. Have we given any token, tangible and real that will encourage those who have fears in their hearts to dispel them and to feel that the future is opening up with bright prospects for them? These are the sort of things we should have in our minds in this House when we are called upon to face any question that has a racial significance.

Stress has been laid in the course of this debate on the economic advantages that have already come to the African and will increasingly come. Stress has been laid upon the educational facilities that have been provided in past years. Disappointment has been expressed that more gratitude has not been shown by those who have received these large educational and other facilities. Well, Mr Speaker, gratitude is, I feel, all too lacking in every community and walk of life in these days, but in the giving of services, in conferring benefits and receiving benefits as the years pass, that very action demands on both sides increased responsibility upon those who provide these facilities that we shall be ready to adjust our outlook on life and our practices in the light of advances that are made. It means that the community of the older civilisation must be prepared to make real changes as soon as a large enough section of the younger civilisation has grown in approaching understanding and responsibility and I would maintain that although granted there is a very large amount of work to be done for the African community in every part of the Federation, there is already a sufficient body emerging from the African community with education, with ideas, with the opportunity to share with us in cultural pursuits that we must realign our whole attitude and plan.

Racial partnership is, of course, a far bigger thing than Post Office counters and railway meals and all of us are, I trust bending our energies to see how best in constructive ways we can advance the Africans within the community to feel that that racial partnership and advance is being guaranteed to them. Practical steps must be demonstrated. It would help the peace and sympathy of our communities in the Federation, if Government would willingly agree to accept an amendment to this motion – To leave out all the words after 'that' and to insert 'in order to exemplify the principle of equal service and opportunity for all sections of the community, Government takes administrative action to ensure (a) that in the Post Offices of the Federation, new buildings should have no racial divisions within and existing Post Office buildings should have racial divisions removed; (b) that all passengers who have paid for first and second class accommodation on the Rhodesian Railways be served in the dining coaches, irrespective of race'.

I repeat and emphasise that these are but practical issues that I think should have been dealt with long ago by administrative action. They are not the whole part of racial partnership which is a thing which is far far better and far far bigger and we must aim at it but these are tokens and would help considerably at the present time.

16th March 1955 No confidence

I maintain that the whole argument of the Honourable member for Kafue [Mr van Eeden] has been to disrupt the Federation and to re-write the Constitution. This is not a time for new schemes. The shape of things to come will be determined by the Government's ability or inability to implement to the full the letter and spirit of the Constitution as committed to us. It is a purpose of equal opportunity for all, irrespective of race. It is a purpose of unity, not of division, of co-operation not of separation. The Honourable member for Kafue is aiming at a division, of territory, a division of potential, a division of political structure, based on race in the ultimate analysis rather than on our common humanity.

Let me refer to the matter of Dominion status referred to by the Honourable member for Kafue. I wish to emphasise that this is a very sore point among the African population of Nyasaland, whom I have the honour to represent. There have been occasions when this matter has been made to appear even by Honourable Ministers of the Federal Government rather an urgent matter. They are doing a grave disservice to any chance that the Federation has of success by toying with the idea of Dominion status. As soon as it is dealt with as a serious issue, the African population not unnaturally begins to say: 'Well then Federation is purely an interim measure until the original and intended thing all along can be achieved'. I feel that the Honourable member for Kafue [Mr van Eeden] was a little unfair to the Constitution and the Preamble thereto when he jumped to the question of Dominion status, without underlining the part that goes before it, where it is clearly stated that this set-up of Federation in particular would 'foster partnership and co-operation between the inhabitants and enable the Federation, when they so desire, to go forward towards the attainment of full membership of the Commonwealth' . . .

. . . The second point I want to take up with the Honourable member for Kafue is that he had not read with sufficient care paragraph 4 of the Preamble to the Constitution in which it is clearly stated that Northern Rhodesia and Nyasaland should continue under the special protection of Her Majesty, Mr Speaker, to be responsible in particular for control of land in these territories and political advancement of the peoples thereof . . .

. . . The third point with which I wish to deal, Mr Speaker, is that I feel there is undue recognition in all that is being said, of the ability that the Africans have and that they should be allowed to use in their advancement in this Federation. The Government needs to be much more definite in its policy of giving every opportunity to Africans according to their ability to provide training to allow them to advance fully. I was disturbed recently to read in a magazine, *Optima*, an article by the Right Honourable the Prime Minister in which he gave the impression that Africans had been pushed forward in Nyasaland just because there were not enough Europeans. This is scarcely fair to the Colonial Office and the Nyasaland Government's policy and the achievement of that policy. There would be far less uneasiness in the minds of the Africans about immigration if it was clearly demonstrated that the Government was fully aware of the potential for skilled service that exists among Africans and recognising the ability of those who have had the opportunity to climb and be trained, press on confidently to extend the field of training and assure that places in all walks of life will be available to the trained personnel . . .

. . . I feel we shall have to be much more prepared to spend money on the higher training of Africans so that they can look to the Federation and its leaders for a full and progressive future . . .

13th August 1956   Status, Federal State

Rev A.B. Doig: Mr Speaker, this proposal that has been put before us for debate at the present time, is, to my mind one that can only be described as an amazingly provocative and highly unnecessary exercise in constitutional manipulation. The Right Honourable the Prime Minister has been quite frank in acknowledging that the approach he has made in these past weeks was badly timed that it was open to misunderstanding in many quarters and that it might prejudice a fully liberal approach to the whole franchise question. If in fact his approach should be turned down by the British Government, these things are serious matters and the responsibility for them must lie with the initiator of the proposals himself.

I want to emphasise the importance of this matter because if there is one thing that needs to be said again and again by those in authority both in the Federal sphere and in other spheres it is that Federation is no temporary expedient for something else but an accepted system for the foreseeable future . . .

. . . The Right Honourable the Prime Minister is asking for technical independence – (Mr Chirwa – What does it mean?) – complete responsibility to be granted to the Federal Government in its own sphere and the reasons given are twofold. The first, I find not very edifying at all. It is not, as I would hope in the future that a claim of Dominion status could be brought forward on the grounds of peace and understanding, partnership and real co-operation but now the reason is – lest in the near future other countries gain a higher status than our own. We are told that the electorate of the Federation just would not stand for this happening and that feelings would run very high. These, Mr Speaker are grave words to come from the Right Honourable the Prime Minister. If they are true, it reveals to us a very serious state of affairs in the electorate of the Federation and of the measure in which they understand the pressing issues of peace and good order and co-operation that are before us.

The editor of *East Africa and Rhodesia*, a staunch supporter and well-wisher of the Federation, pleading for patience in this very matter of Dominion status has said: 'There are more important matters than artificial prestige' and I believe and hope that the bulk of the electors will agree with him . . .

. . . I would point out in all seriousness that the effect of the Right Honourable the Prime Minister's proposal has been to cast doubts on what should have been inherently clear in its own wording and not subject to any personal opinion or recollection and if this sort of thing is going to be possible it is bound to undermine what confidence exists in the proposals, the Constitution, on which we are now working for the establishment of a comprehensive state. The last paragraph of the Preamble, Mr Speaker, to my mind, sets us a vision and a task, the establishment of a State that will have internal security, that will be characterised by its outstanding advancement both in economic matters and in personal relationships, that will demonstrate more than mere words can ever do what partnership really means and that will be outstandingly co-operative in its endeavour. That is a vision and a task and the goal beyond it, with united desire and acclaim, full membership of the Commonwealth.

16th July 1957 Constitutional Amendment

On the face of it, this is simply a measure to increase the size of this Federal Assembly. This is a proposal that can be judged purely on efficiency of working and adequacy of representation. After I have listened to all the reasons for increasing the size of the House, I find myself unconvinced as to its necessity and wisdom at the present time.

I pass to the question that has already been referred to in the representation or the additional representation of Africans in this Assembly, as proposed in this Bill. I find it rather disturbing that the African members from the Northern Territories are now to be put in two different categories and one naturally begins to ask why. The Honourable Minister gave us some indication of the purpose behind it in seeking some new system of election which would not be purely on racial grounds but anything that he said was mild compared to the enlargement offered upon it by the Honourable member, Mr Davies. I hope that in the reasons that the Honourable member Mr Davies gave for his departure from what I consider to be a fundamental principle of representation in the Constitution, I hope he considered very carefully the effect that his words were going to have in the Northern Territories.

I say in all seriousness, Sir, that I can think of no speech that has been so damaging to the prospects of Federation in the Northern territories than some of the remarks made by the Honourable member Mr Davies. The groupings in the Bill of the African members could, of course, be used quite fairly by making all four in each Northern territory be elected by a communal electoral roll or by following some system of election by a body chosen by the Governor of the territory, as is at present the method of election, but I feel, Sir, that there has been sufficient indication given that that is not the intention of the Government and that I must therefore warn the Government that if the new African posts from the North were to be elected by any body or electoral roll that was not predominantly African, that would amount in my opinion to a breach of faith on the part of the Federal Government and incidentally on the part of the United Kingdom Government, if the latter were prepared to accept it . . .

. . . Mr Chairman, I indicated earlier on I felt it was very important in a matter of this kind that if there was a measure of agreement on the ultimate objectives that one should consider very carefully whether any steps contemplated in the interim would assist towards or lessen the chances of success in the ultimate objective and the Honourable Minister himself has indicated that he recognises that the proposals that Government has in mind will in fact produce a situation in which two of the African members from each of the Northern Territories would in fact be returned by a roll on which Africans will be very much in the minority. Does the Honourable Minister not realise that that is bound in the nature of things – by the past and present attitude of the African to Federation – to result in an intensified racial approach to politics and to this House?

8th January 1958   Electoral Bill

Mr Speaker, these are the points on which I take my stand in opposition to this Bill: that it is lessening African influence; that it is a poor demonstration of the extent to which the franchise should be extended to Africans in choosing their representatives and that it has engendered suspicions that should never have been aroused so early in the history of the Federation as to what things are certain and what things can be changed. I have always maintained that it was absolutely important for the life and future of the Federation that there should be a considerable period of constitutional stability. That stability has been upset. It has been upset by the initiative of the Federal Government and the consequences must lie with them. (Applause)

Chapter 6

Involved with the Academics

In the middle of my political life, there was another field in which I took great joy and satisfaction and ever found cause for hope. I had been appointed in 1953 to serve on the committee to plan for a university college for the Rhodesias and Nyasaland. This seemed to me to be a vital contribution to the future of the territories, whatever relationship they might continue to develop. If anything could help, surely a university centre, with carefully chosen and dedicated staff, with the freedom of learning for which a university has always contended, would have a powerful impact on the living and thinking of all races passing through its doors.

The University College was created and was soon active. We were so fortunate in the staff we attracted from the United Kingdom and under the principalship of Dr Walter Adams, great progress was made. For some seven or eight years, I served on the University Council and took part in all its deliberations. We were constantly battling against the ingrained prejudice of the community in Southern Rhodesia. I had regretted that Salisbury was chosen as the site of the University but went along with the decision in the confident expectation that the University would have stronger influence on the life of Southern Rhodesia than the other way round. We had to contend with the Southern Rhodesian practice of separate racial accommodation and life but in the end we won through for an integrated system of life on the campus.

It was a great day, in 1957, when the Queen Mother was installed as President of the University College. I was thrilled to be invited, as a member of the Council to open the proceedings with prayer.

God is great and greatly to be praised. There is no searching of His understanding.

Eternal and Ever Blessed God, the God and Father of our Lord Jesus Christ, we offer Thee our worship and our praise, for that Thou art the Lord and Giver of life, the Creator and Sustainer of men. Visit us anew this day with Thy salvation and strengthen us by Thy Spirit.

Almighty God, Ruler and Judge of all men, we thank Thee,

Installation of the Queen Mother as President of University College.

who hast called Thy servant, Elizabeth our Queen, to rule over a great family of nations, in many lands, of many languages. Bestow upon her, we pray Thee, abundantly of Thy grace that she may carry her heavy responsibilities without fear and that under her gracious reign, the whole nation may be established in righteousness and peace to the glory of Thy name and the increase of Thy Kingdom throughout the world.

Grant to Thy servant, Elizabeth, the Queen Mother, Thy sustaining presence in these days of constant travel and demanding duty among us, that all her works may be fruitful in blessing and that Thy peace may garrison her heart.

O God, source of all light and truth, we pray for this University College, giving Thee thanks for all whose experience and generosity have enabled us to progress thus far. We praise Thee that through the ages, Thou hast inspired men to seek and in seeking to find so that we are the heirs of a great heritage of scholarship and discovery.

Bless, we pray Thee, this new centre of learning, all who teach and all who are taught, that here, by teaching and research, the frontiers of knowledge may be extended; that from this place, the Governments, professions and industries of our State may be serviced by leaders of sound judgement and tried learning; and grant, O God, that with all increase of knowledge, there may be a deepening of adoration and worship towards Thee, who art the Creator, and in whom alone, all things are carried to their fulfilment.

These things we ask in the name and for the sake of Jesus Christ, our Lord, to whom, with Thee, O Father and the Holy Spirit, be praise and glory, world without end.

Amen

The speeches were full of a consciousness of great things begun, to be carried forward to an increasingly glorious future. The rich promise and expectation was underlined by the remarkable gathering of distinguished scholars and administrators from universities and colleges around the world. As the years have passed, these hopes have been more than fulfilled. I have kept in touch and with the appointment of the Rev Robert Craig, a Church of Scotland minister as principal in succession to Walter Adams, I was given a continual up-date of the University's affairs.

I recall with joy this crucial contact with an institution of such importance and significance.

Chapter 7

Back to Crucial Work with the Church

After a few months at home, we returned to Nyasaland in February 1959. The months at home were full of activity and interest. I addressed meetings to explain what I had been doing over the past years and I marvelled at the tremendous support there was in the Church of Scotland for all we had been saying and doing. I had time at Westminster with prominent members of both main parties. My special favourite was Iain McLeod whom I was to meet again later in Nyasaland as he opened the way for Nyasaland to come out of the Federation.

We returned with great joy to the full-time service of the Church. I suppose I took pleasure in disproving the critical comments of some of my colleagues who, in 1953 said, 'That's the end of Doig in the Mission. He will not return.' It had always been my expectation to return, after what I saw as a temporary deviation to meet a special need.

I was delighted to be given responsibility as General Secretary of the Blantyre Synod of the Church of Central Africa Presbyterian. This was a key post, with the special task of training two African colleagues to take over from me in that imaginative process of indigenisation of the CCAP, in which I had been involved for years past. My two colleagues and assistants were the Rev Jonathan Sangaya as Assistant

General Secretary and Mr Durbin Nkwaila as Assistant Education Secretary. We were a happy and united team and soon made such progress that some two years later, I was able to hand over to them their separate responsibilities and retreat to the back office, where I was assistant to them.

In addition, I was involved in the developing work of the Nyasaland Christian Council, a meaningful association of churches that did much for the educational and medical contribution of missions and strengthened the evangelistic witness of the churches. Here too, the Africans were taking their full share in planning and in representation. It had seemed to me from a long time back, that it was vitally important that, as we spoke forcibly on the increased opportunity for Africans in the affairs of state, so we should have visible and practical signs in the Church of their advancement and valuable leadership.

Of course, I should make it clear that the Church of Central Africa, Presbyterian had been completely self-governing since away back in 1923, and the driving force in the work of evangelism had progressively passed to the African ministers and evangelists in the intervening years. Still, there had remained an apparent predominance of missionaries in many spheres and posts and indeed, the Blantyre Mission Council had continued to function, entirely consisting of missionaries and dealing with such important activities as educational and medical work. Some years back, the Mission Council had been scrapped and the missionaries had become fully ministers and members of the CCAP. Now we were moving to the final visible transfer of power and initiative to the African.

I also had the care of the English-speaking congregation in Blantyre and rejoiced to see the attendance increase with members from all language communities. We stayed in the manse in Blantyre. Barbara played a lively part in the work of the Mvano (The Woman's Guild) and had opportunity once again to apply her teaching skills as a member of the staff of the Kapeni Teacher Training College. Peter and Isabelle had a happy time at school and we had the most marvellous birthday parties for them in the manse garden in November (Peter) and March (Isabelle).

Yet life was not too easy or plain-sailing. The rising resistance of the African to the continued Federation, the increased excitement in the return of Dr Banda to lead the Independence Movement, led to demonstrations and hard words from both Congress and Government. Government produced stories of a plot to endanger European lives and to overthrow the Government. Unfortunately, the Federal forces had to play a large part in maintaining law and order and this led to a deterioration rather than to any improvement in the situation.

We recall an occasion, when we made our way as a family to Mlanje. As we entered the tea-growing area, we were held up by a road block. The Africans were in action to protest against the attitudes of various tea planters. As we stopped, we heard them make threats against our children. While anxious, we immediately began talking to them in Cewa. The situation was transformed. They recognised who we were. The grim faces lit up with smiles and we were soon conscious of that deep warmth of feeling and belonging together that we had always known. We went on our way, rejoicing and hopeful.

In this connection, I could profitably quote here what was written by the editor of *Life and Work*, some twenty years later, when I was nominated as Moderator of the General Assembly of the Church of Scotland. R.D. Kernohan came out on a fact finding visit when things were growing difficult in Nyasaland.

In 1981 he wrote:

I first met Andrew Doig 20 years before, when I am sure he had no more thoughts of being Moderator than I had of being a church editor. It was in Blantyre. Dr Banda was waiting to win the elections. The country was uneasy but expectant.

We never know till too late what a good or bad lasting

impression we can make on others, when face to face with the unexpected. My lasting memory of Andrew Doig was of the calm air and authority which he showed at what, for him, may have been a routine police check on the road back into Blantyre. I remembered the air of courteous authority better than anything he said.

In the Blantyre Mission in 1959, we were very much involved in a deteriorating situation. On the one hand, we were contacted by the Provincial Commissioner to accept young Aleke Banda, sent back from Southern Rhodesia, as our guest at the Mission. This we gladly did. On the other hand, Government officers were too ready to accuse us of an over sympathetic response to what the protestors were saying. Then there came the Declaration of a State of Emergency and hundreds of our prominent and highly educated Nyasalanders were taken into detention. This resulted in a crisis in our educational work.

As Education Secretary, I had to try to keep our secondary school going, by using wives of missionaries as staff and standing in myself to teach mathematics in preparation for the end of session exams. The results, when they came, a high percentage of passes, brought us all great joy.

In another area, I was able to use my past involvement in national and political affairs, to insist that I be allowed to visit the detainees wherever they were. This was a marvellous ministry. I travelled to centres in Southern Rhodesia, at Gwelo for example and to detention camps in Nyasaland. I was impressed. There was no sense of depression. The detainees were busy in correspondence courses on history, political science and economics, preparing consciously for that day they knew would dawn, when they would be in positions of power in their own country. I had long and profitable sessions with Dr Banda in Gwelo. There were present also his immediate and key officers. I responded to a request from the detainees that I should produce a scheme of Bible Study for them. They wanted it built around these key questions – 'What is man? What is freedom? and what is the role of the Church in these spheres?'

I was able to be a go-between for detainees and their families and to speak forcibly with the Nyasaland Government about the implications for the future of the detainees and of their dedication to prepare for power. I had the chance to develop my relationship and understanding of Dr Banda whom I had known for many years from the days when he was a doctor in London. I had read with interest his booklet written in conjunction with Nkumbula against the idea of Federation and had benefitted from his comments on the speeches I had made and my actions in the Nyasaland Legislative Council in opposing the imposition of Federation. I had discussed, as indicated earlier, the relationship of my resignation from the Federal Assembly to his return to lead the Independence Movement. Now I was in a new position, seeing him respond with dignity to his enforced detention. I saw him plan with determination his own hopes for the future, saw him promoting and preparing the younger men around him for the demands that would be made upon them in years to come. He was a complex character was Banda, subject to moods and excesses in judgement and violent in his reaction to individuals who did not respond to his views and hopes. I had fears for a continued balanced leadership in the long term. Yet I recognised in him the man for the hour, as far as Nyasaland was concerned.

His hour came. The British Government recognised that it could not hold the Federation together. After the brilliant visit of Iain McLeod, Nyasaland and Northern Rhodesia were allowed to opt out and Southern Rhodesia went its own way. It was a great regret to me that the British Government did not have the strength of will to overhaul radically the Constitution of Southern Rhodesia at the same time. However, it was to be a delay of only a few years after the agony of Smith's unilateral independence move that Southern Rhodesia also faced a new future under Mugabe.

In Nyasaland, Dr Banda formed his government and independence was assured. We had high hopes of the success of such a good team of ministers as Banda had assembled following the 1962 Act. Unfortunately, these hopes were not fulfilled as some of the ablest of Banda's ministers had to leave the country for their own safety.

On the church side, I was able to press on with the transfer of responsibility to Jonathan and Durbin. Early in 1962, I became Assistant General Secretary and they took up their posts as General Secretary and Education Secretary. I moved into the back office.

As time went on, I began to consider whether the time had not come to make a dramatic change of ministry and return to Scotland. I had a fear that there might be a suspicion that the man in the back office still called the tune, I would not for worlds have seen any lessening of the victory we had achieved in African advancement and leadership.

So I intimated that I would not be returning after leave in October 1962. The Africans were most generous in their tributes which did not make the decision any easier. We could look back on such a wonderful record of service through the years since I arrived in 1939 that it was a wrench to think of leaving for the unknown that might await us in the parishes of Scotland. The fact that Peter was now 10 and Isabelle 7 made it easier for there could be real advantage for them in making the educational change at such a time.

We had a great send off as we started our journey to Beira and then by ship, on the East Coast route through Kenya, the Red Sea, Egypt and Italy back to Britain.

I had a moving goodbye from the Governor, Glyn Jones who thanked us and wished us well. It is interesting to reflect on the relationships I had with Governors. With Geoffrey Colby, I had an easy understanding and a very meaningful mutual respect. With Robert Armitage, I never felt at ease. No doubt this stems from the fact that I knew and he knew that he had been appointed to see that Federation was accepted and endured. To him, I must have seemed an awkward presence, complicating his task. I could not agree with the attitude he took to circumstances that ended in the Declaration of a State of Emergency. With Glyn Jones, we had a different character altogether. He had a warmth of feeling and a deep concern for the new Malawi that was to arise and fulfilled his role with dignity and with grace.

Chapter 8

The Parish Ministry

We reached Scotland in October 1962 and were soon happily settled in the furlough house at Comely Bank. We faced an extensive programme of deputation work throughout Scotland, which we thoroughly enjoyed. Congregations were so interested in the situation we had left and the future as we saw it.

I did not rush around, looking for a kirk. I was patient, eager to feel led by God to the next sphere of service, praying that it would gather up in some special way all that I had done up to that moment.

Amazingly, I was invited to apply for the vacant parish of St John's and King's Park, Dalkeith, was selected as sole nominee and inducted in May 1963. I was thrilled. Here was a large lively gathering of God's people, some 850 in number, with a dedicated band of office-bearers and plenty of young life in Sunday School, Bible Class and Youth Organisations. As a congregation, they were proud of their history and during my time there, they celebrated their centenary. There was a strong interest in the Overseas Work of the Church and Barbara and I were made to feel that they wanted to hear about our doings over the years. I was delighted in my early months at Dalkeith to be invited to take a broadcast service to coincide with the celebration of the Independence of Malawi. The choir eagerly played their part in the service as they sang in the Cewa language, the hymn 'Bwenzi lathu ndiye Yesu' (What a friend we have in Jesus).

The demands of visitation, both in hospital and in the homes were considerable but I enjoyed them. I was made to feel welcome in the homes and systematically covered the congregation in the company of the district elders. They were good enough to make it plain that, though they expected full service and commitment from me, they would understand that there would be outside links and engagements I would want to undertake following upon my overseas service. So I was a member of the Overseas Council, Chairman of the Christian Aid Committee, member of the Christian Aid Board in London, on the Committee of the United Society for Christian Literature and on the Board of the National Bible Society of Scotland.

It was a great joy and challenge when I was invited to become, in 1965, the Clerk to the Presbytery of Dalkeith. I did hesitate, wondering if I could cope with the extra duties. Perhaps I was even more provoked by the minister who phoned to say he was opposing my appointment on the grounds that he could not understand how one who had been twenty-five years in the Church in Africa, could possibly cope with the procedures of the Church of Scotland. Laughingly, I explained to him all that had been involved in being Senior Clerk to the Synod of Blantyre in Malawi. I don't think he was entirely convinced but I have to say that I had no more loyal supporter than himself through all my years as Clerk.

Being a Presbytery Clerk, is a demanding task. It is not just the mass of paper work that must be done and the need to be precise in one's rulings within the Presbytery. It is much more the personal element that figures so prominently. The Clerk has no authority to intervene in the way his fellow ministers act or fail to act. He is essentially the servant of the Court that appointed him. It is amazing, though, how that servant status can add up to a wonderful opportunity to live with an open ear to the needs and problems of one's colleagues and in strict confidence to help to carry their burdens. Any Presbytery

Clerk worth his salt will treasure the confidence placed in him by his fellows.

One of the great joys that Barbara and I shared was to try to be a welcome and support to the young ministers and their wives who joined the Presbytery. We used to organise a social for them. It deepened the fellowship and widened the contacts. Through the years we have kept in touch with these young couples and rejoiced to see their ministries develop.

Being Presbytery Clerk meant that I was a member of the General Assembly every year. I had lots of Assembly contacts over the years through the work of the Overseas Council but this was a new door of opportunity. It widened my contribution, through the debates, and through service on the Records Committee of the Assembly, where I served as Convener for several years. It was all to add up to an increased feeling of confidence, when the day came that I had to preside over the Assembly as Moderator, though that was still some ten to fifteen years ahead.

Our years in Dalkeith were specially memorable, for that was where we found ourselves increasingly as a family unit. Peter and Isabelle were happy in the manse. They developed steadily through activity in church and at school. We were thrilled when they both won places in the Merchant Company Schools (Peter in Stewarts and Isabelle in George Watsons Ladies). We would not have thought of it until David Clelland, an elder and a headmaster, counselled us that there could be disadvantages for children of the manse having their schooling locally. Our appreciation of the decision to enter them for admission to the Merchant Company Schools grew as we saw the greatly increased life and contacts they made there, side by side with their identification locally through the church and Sunday School and Bible Class and Youth Fellowship. They played their full part there and both of them held office in the Youth Fellowship. It was good for the congregation to see the whole family involved in its work.

Barbara revitalised the women's side of the congregation not only through the Guild where she presided so effectively but also by the creation of a Coffee Morning – a gathering that provided opportunity for friendship and discovery by locals and visitors alike. The fee was ridiculously low at sixpence per head. Barbara insisted that there was no sale of goods or raffle tickets allowed. The meeting was for fellowship and introductions and it was brilliantly successful. The suggestion for such a gathering was put to the Session and approved. One elder, William Toynbee, came to Barbara and said, 'Go ahead and try but remember if it seems at any stage to flag in interest or effectiveness, stop it and try something else.' It was wise advice but we rejoice to know that some twenty-five years later, the Coffee Morning is still flourishing.

We had such a marvellous band of leaders and helpers in youth work, in the Guides, the Boys' Brigade and the Sunday School. In the Primary Sunday School, we had Sadie Lamb, wife of one of our elders as leader. Her early death was a shattering blow to us all. In the upper school, we were greatly helped by Susan Cowell, now a minister of the Kirk. It had been our custom, in company with so many others, to close our Sunday School from June to September. Susan had other ideas. She put it like this. 'Holiday period? But God doesn't take a holiday.' So under her leadership, we devised a summer Children's Church, to keep the challenge and inspiration of the Gospel sounding forth for the young all the year through.

It was at Dalkeith that we had our marvellous summer holidays, especially in the setting of Keil Point at Southend in Argyll. We were happily housed by Mrs McSporran and enjoyed the fun and friendship on the local golf course at Dunaverty. Peter had his first lessons in golf at Machrihanish from the professional. We also launched forth on out caravanning exploits, greatly enjoying towing the van to Oban, Lochinver, and Achmelvik to mention but a few. In his last two years at school, Peter joined the grouse beaters at Glen Quaich near Amulree and we used to go up to see him. Both Peter and Isabelle were adventurous as they paid visits to Europe in small groups with friends or in the Crusader outing to Morocco in which Isabelle shared.

It was also while at Dalkeith, in 1963, that we completed our family by making contact with Anne. She was the child that was born to Nan just before her death. She had been brought up by her mother's sister, Isa and her husband, Jim Smith. Against much resistance, we had sought to get to know her and were at last successful. She became a regular member of the family. Peter and Isabelle early on made the stipulation that there was to be no nonsense about a step-sister. She was their sister and we have enjoyed seeing the links grow between the three of them, as the years passed. Barbara and Anne established a real understanding and Barbara was marvellous in her care and concern for Anne.

The manse, 51 Eskbank Road was, of course, the only manse we have occupied in Scotland. We greatly enjoyed the house, with its many rooms and large garden. I used to joke that I could look after the congregation or the garden but not both. Still we managed to keep the garden tidy and made the house a centre of hospitality for many from overseas.

I was 48 when I went to Dalkeith. We were happy through the years. There's something very special about being a parish minister. You have a key role to play in the community and in the congregation. You are made to feel that you are trusted and that they expect great things from you. I was welcomed in the life of the Newbattle Golf Club and found my position as chaplain to King's Park School a constant delight. We had two great traditions in St John's and King's Park Church. The one was an annual Jumble Sale. We had a reputation for having the best jumble of any and the hall was packed to capacity. They tell me there were bargains to be had but what always astonished me was the energy and enthusiasm put into it by the office-bearers and women members of the congregation, who set up the tables, decided on the prices, rigidly controlled the would-be shoplifters and packed up and cleaned up when all was done. The second was the Annual Garden Fete, held in someone's grounds. What preparation went into setting the scene. What a variety of pursuits there was! How effective were the stalls of goods for sale and how marvellous the provision of music to match the occasion. The profit was not most of all in terms of cash but of fellowship and fun.

There were many memorable services through the years. Professor James S. Stewart favoured us with one of his matchless sermons on the occasion of our centenary. Once a year, the Youth Fellowship conducted a complete morning service. Barbara and I took pride in these services and not least when Peter and Isabelle played their parts in them. Office-bearers shared in the reading of Scripture at the morning service. On Christmas Eve, the church was packed, a glorious evangelistic opportunity, for many were there who had never darkened a church door or who had allowed the joy of the Gospel to become absent from their lives. For the morning services, I tried to meet the needs of the children with an address before they left for Sunday School. For the congregation, I often presented a series of sermons on a theme extending over several weeks.

Chapter 9

Let the Word Speak

At 57, my way seemed set for years to come, happily serving in a congregation I had grown to love with the added interest of a share in the problems and decisions of all the churches in the Presbytery.

Then in 1972, there came an invitation from the National Bible Society of Scotland to consider taking up office as their General Secretary. Was this a stepping outside of the Church as I had known it and loved it? Then there came deeper thoughts. What about my conviction through the years that we were led from one experience to another, to gather up the fruits we had gained for a new and greater endeavour ahead? Did not this invitation gather up my joy in preaching the Word with all I had learned through the years, of the importance of having the Scriptures in every possible language, as I had seen by serving with the troops in the Army and as I was constantly aware of in my missionary work in Malawi.

I decided this was a new and wider way of service for the remaining years of my ministry and I accepted the invitation. I have never regretted it. The congregation of St John's and King's Park were graciousness itself in understanding and support.

So we planned to move to Edinburgh, found a suitable house in Craiglea Drive and purchased it, thanks to a hundred per cent loan from the Society.

I was appointed from 1st September 1972 and that very month was introduced to the work in a dramatic way. I was to attend the meeting of the United Bible Societies' Council in Addis Ababa. They had not arranged it for my benefit but it felt like that. It was strange to return to Addis after a gap of twenty-nine years but more important was to find myself in company with the key figures in the Bible Society movement from all over the world. I was made to feel at home among them and I sensed the honoured place given to the National Bible Society of Scotland as one of the four original founding Bible Societies. The others were the American Bible Society, the Netherlands Bible Society and the British and Foreign Bible Society, all of them having originated in the early days of the nineteenth century. I was aware of the growth through the years, whereby there were now over a hundred Bible Societies, planning together the communication of the Word for the World. I thrilled to the advance from some part of the Scriptures in sixty-four languages to the 1,600 total being handled in translation, production and distribution in 1972. I really had come into a very large place and looked forward to growing friendships and increased involvement in this world-wide task.

The choice of title for the Council meeting was a very happy one – LET THE WORD SPEAK – and how very often I was to ring the changes on that theme through the succeeding years.

As General Secretary, in Scotland, I had a special place in the European scene. I was soon a member of the Executive Committee for Europe and was delighted to discover they had a plan of meeting in a different capital of Europe each year. So began a new discovery of people and places in Brussels, Madrid, Oslo, Helsinki, Copenhagen, and Belgrade. Usually it meant arriving, attending meetings and departing again with no time to explore. There was one notable exception. When I phoned to book my passage for five days in Oslo, the travel agency indicated that it would be £160 for five days, but if I could stay for six days, there was a special fare of £80. Joyfully, I booked for the six days, had one day entirely free for sightseeing, with the satisfaction of knowing that I had saved the Bible Society money.

There was joy of another kind when I flew to Budapest. We touched down in Vienna and had to wait in the transit lounge for the onward flight. When the call to board came, I took my leisurely way to the barrier, only to be told that the flight was full.

'How could it be?' I asked, 'I have a transit card.'

'Oh, sorry,' they said, 'but we have overbooked.'

I argued the point and tried to persuade them that the most serious international situation would develop if I did not arrive in Budapest by that plane.

At last, they took me out to the plane, showed me that every seat was occupied and then said, 'There is only one way for you to reach Budapest by this plane. That is, if you are prepared to sit on a box, between the two pilots up front all the way.'

Trying to look shocked, I was inwardly delighted. All the way to Budapest, I had a magnificent view, with the highly informed comments of both pilots as we travelled. I was treated to coffee and sweets all the way and whisked off the plane before everyone else when we arrived.

I told my story to Bertalan Tamas at the Scottish Mission in Budapest. He was as thrilled as I was and I've heard him tell the story on many occasions to others to show how highly Bible Society staff are thought of wherever they go.

Barbara and I were able to share travelling overseas twice to our great enrichment.

Poland

We crossed the Channel and went by train from the Hook of Holland on the Moscow Express all the way to Warsaw. It was a good journey.

We were served tea at frequent intervals by the attendant who spoke little English but grinned all over his face as he disgorged little packets from his pocket, saying, 'Sugar?' We arrived at Warsaw exactly on time, which greatly impressed us and had a most warm-hearted welcome from my opposite number, Barbara Narzynska, Bible Society Secretary and wife of the Lutheran Bishop. We were accommodated in their town residence with a gracious woman to look after us. She knew no English, but everything we required was supplied with joy and courtesy and concern for our welfare. There were no signs of a bedroom but we soon realised that the place was used mainly for receptions and that any one of the many settees could be pulled out to provide a bed, large and comfortable.

As we were just over the wall from the Roman Catholic Cardinal's house, we were very much in the church scene.

We rejoiced in Bible House in Novy Swiat, the building that survived the destruction during the war, when the whole centre of Warsaw was destroyed. In wonder we gazed at the re-built city, just as it had been. We travelled widely with Barbara, having our attention drawn to things we would never have noticed as ordinary tourists. We visited the shrine of the Black Madonna at Chestachowa. We wandered through Krakov and feasted on strawberries which were just on their short season.

At Auschwitz, we were strangely silent and deeply moved as we read the story and recognised the signs of the unspeakable horrors that were perpetrated in the concentration camp. We accepted the reality of the place 'where no bird sings'. Our eyes were held by a young girl, just along the road from Auschwitz, clad in white on her way to her confirmation and first communion. In very deed, light and life were springing forth in the very place of death. It was a privilege to visit Auschwitz in the company of Barbara Narzynska for she had her own story to tell. Her father was Secretary of the Bible Society before her. He and his wife were in grave danger during the war, being picked up by the Germans. Her mother could have been freed if she had claimed that she was German but she would not. Several times her father just escaped the gas chambers. Her mother jumped from a train, being taken she knew not where. In her jump she was injured, but after months out of touch, she turned up at the family 'house in the forest' outside Warsaw. She lived to be a very old woman.

We were very conscious of the deep spirituality experienced and expressed by the Polish people. We came away with a great respect for them and a realisation and admiration for the survival potential of the Polish people through many gruelling centuries.

The effective organisation of Bible House in Warsaw was impressive and we saw at first hand the needs we sought to meet through the fellowship and finance of the United Bible Societies. We saw the queues, seeking the Illustrated New Testament in Polish, which at that time had just gone out of print, to the great distress of those who had travelled long distances to obtain a copy.

I commented on the display of the Bible in Esperanto and confessed my ignorance of its existence. Barbara Narzynska took great delight in quietly commenting: 'How surprising! It was produced by the National Bible Society of Scotland.' I concealed my embarrassment as best I could while vowing to bring myself up to date with the doings of the Society before I came on the scene.

All in all, Poland was a very special place in our recollection and esteem. We enjoyed friendship, music (Chopin and others) and a very special and varied introduction to the history of a great people.

Africa

Our other shared tour was to Africa, where I was to see something of the translation work of the United Bible Societies in Kenya, Malawi, and Zambia. Each country was special.

In Kenya, I was returning to a land I knew and served in during the war. It was a joy to introduce Barbara to people and places I had known. We travelled extensively all the way to Nakuru on the one side and to Nanyuki and Chogoria on the other. We were in the good hands of Yohana Mbogori, the Bible Society Secretary, who guided us around. Through him we were immediately in touch with the people and even invited to a wedding at which the young couple had to endure two addresses given by Yohana and myself. We called on the Rev Charles Muhoro of the Presbyterian Church in East Africa. He was now retired but was eager and delighted to meet me again after the passage of thirty years since we were Army Chaplains together in the East Africa Command. It was a joy to renew acquaintance with the Rev John Gatu, General Secretary of the Presbyterian Church in East Africa and with him to see something of the growing activity and influence of the Church. We also spent time with that brilliant translator of the Scriptures into the Maasai language, John Mpaayei.

Going to Malawi was, of course, like going home. Here we were able to sit down with the Inter-Confessional team and clearly understand what they were saying in Cewa. It was fascinating to listen to them, teasing out words and phrases to let them speak more powerfully than the long-standing Union Nyanja version was able to do. One day they were working on the words 'The Grace of our Lord Jesus Christ' seeking to find the exact connotation of Grace. They noted the word Cisomo in the Union Nyanja version and found its meaning as 'that which draws or attracts' to be inadequate. They passed on to the word Kwaulere as used in the current Roman Catholic translation. It means 'the utterly undeserved gift'. They passed from this also in favour of the phrase Kukoma mtima which means that complete combination of word and action in loving self-giving to another, the act of salvation in which there are no reservations and no contradictions. We felt deeply stirred and satisfied.

This was our first visit to Malawi since we had left it fourteen years previously, visiting and preaching in the churches we used to know. We rejoiced to be present at a graduation ceremony at the Malawi University in Zomba, where among so many others we knew, the child of a student of Barbara's was receiving her degree. Malawians are happy people. They communicate and they share. We felt at once at home but were greatly saddened to miss the young ministers in Banda's Government that we had known and who were now in exile. We were graciously received by the Life President, Dr H. Kamuzu Banda and by his hostess, Mama Kadzamira. It was great to be in close association again with the Rev Jonathan Sangaya and to learn from him of the steady growth of the Church throughout the country.

In Zambia, we made immediate rapport with Chipo Moonga, the Bible Society Secretary, and Dr Jake Lowen, the United Bible Societies Translations Consultant. Jake was an American, a great guy, as they would say – in everything except his driving. He scared the living daylights out of us, as we tore along Zambia's roads. He would find himself coming up to a huge lorry, throwing up great clouds of dust. Before we knew where we were, he would be penetrating the dust cloud with no way of knowing whether anything was coming in the opposite direction. Mercifully, there never was an oncoming vehicle. Soon we relaxed, trusting him fully, for he really handled his vehicle magnificently.

We met with translation teams in various places but our most memorable was when we called in on Donald Siwale, translator of the Cinamwanga Bible, in Northern Zambia. He was in his bwalo (courtyard), when we arrived. He was sitting in the sunshine, reading the modern translation of the New Testament in German. 'I was just checking up,' he said, 'to see how they had dealt with this passage.' I was lost in admiration of his skill and dedication. It is just one striking example of the outstanding ability of the men we draw into translation work. I was delighted to find a personal link with Donald Siwale. He asked if I had been in the army in East Africa. When I agreed that I had, he commented, 'It is good to meet again. I came as a member of a delegation from Zambia in 1942, to Nairobi to seek to improve the communication of members of the armed forces with their families back home. You were among a number of Army officers that we met to work out a scheme together. It is good to meet again after all these years.'

So here we were talking again most meaningfully about communication, the word that God speaks to His children. There was urgency about it. Donald Siwale was in his nineties and he had a dream. Before he died, he wanted to present a copy of his new translation in Cinamwanga to the President of Zambia, Dr Kenneth Kaunda, himself a staunch believer. Donald Siwale made it plain that the issue of his dream rested with me, and the National Bible Society of Scotland. 'Produce the book before I die,' he said and then added as an afterthought, 'but if not, up there I shall know when it happens and rejoice with you.' He was in the world of communication again, the nearness of earth to heaven. I am glad to record that the book was produced in time for him to present it to the President.

The task at home

When I became General Secretary of the National Bible Society of Scotland, there were two urgent tasks laid upon me. One was to find a new headquarters for the Society and sell the historic building in St Andrews Square. The other was to open a new and exciting relationship between the Society and the churches in Scotland.

For the new headquarters, we were thinking of finding a redundant church to be converted. Our Finance Committee set itself to the task and soon we had an objective in view – to acquire the now empty Wester Coates Church. We had architects advice on how it could be altered. I approached the General Trustees to agree on an appropriate figure to be paid, assuming they would be interested in the building being acquired for such a church related purpose. Alas, they had set themselves to advertise and dispose of it to the highest bidder. We put in an offer but the award went to a commercial concern, dependent on their gaining planning permission for the scheme they had in mind. Our son, Peter, who by this time was well on in his studies as an architect, was able to keep his eye on the planning permission aspect. He reported to me that the firm had not been successful. I immediately phoned up the Church Offices and surprised them by telling them what they had only just heard. I asked if we could now talk about a sale by mutual agreement. They insisted on the bidding process all over again.

This time we were successful. In all our discussions in our Finance Committee, and especially in regard to the sale of St Andrews Square, we were greatly indebted to Mr A. Fraser McLennan, an Edinburgh lawyer of great distinction, an elder of the Kirk and with considerable know-how in finance. He was indispensable. He introduced us to Ross Duncan, an Edinburgh architect, who set to work to plan the transformation of the Kirk. By a strange coincidence, Peter had just shortly before started working for Ross Duncan. So around the conference table, discussing the plans, I found myself dealing not only with Scott Duncan but with my son, Peter. They did a great job and we finished with a remarkable refit for the building, giving us three floors within the Church building and ample room for all our staff and work. It cost some £200,000 but this had to be set against the £770,000 we received for St Andrews Square. That left a healthy balance, so that, as had been intended, the change of headquarters was most beneficial to the Bible cause world-wide.

The other task was to relate the Bible Society to all the churches in Scotland. The task was two-fold. We had to serve as the channel through which Scotland's generosity and prayerful support for the world-wide availability of the Word might be ensured. But also, we had to have an increasing regard for the urgent need in Scotland to make the Bible central to all our church worship and mission.

So we stepped up our presentation of the constant and growing needs in so many lands and languages. My own overseas journeys and contacts enabled me to give personal emphasis to the opportunities and I set myself to be heard constantly in the pulpits throughout Scotland in the interests of the Bible cause. It was a delight to have this countrywide connection with the churches of every denomination and to see the fruits of the contacts in increased income and support.

By our publications and productions, we increased awareness of what Bible use had to offer to individual and congregation. We offered a wide range of selections of Scripture for special evangelistic and pastoral ministry. We welcomed the opportunity year by year to be received and heard in all the Church Assemblies in the land. At local level, we stepped up our branches of the Society and were able to involve more and more people. Our essay and painting competitions were eagerly taken up throughout Scotland and this ensured a new and valuable link and service with the younger generation. The background to all this activity was in the existence of the new Bible House and the team of dedicated staff that it was such a joy to lead. The Bible shop ensured a warmth of welcome to all who came to enquire, to purchase and to be helped. We received all as partners with us in a great and worthwhile enterprise. We could put on exhibitions and visual presentations to which came groups of young people and members of the Woman's Guild.

We were thrilled when the Queen expressed her interest in visiting Bible House. We had everything ready when word reached us that illness would prevent her coming, but that the Princess Anne would deputise for her. Her visit was a huge success and we were greatly impressed how, with the short notice she had, she had prepared herself to ask important questions and make apt comment on so many aspects of our work.

Our governing body, the Board, and all our committees were fully representative of the churches and this diversity was also present in our staff.

The key position occupied by our Society through the years gave us a special place in United Bible Societies conferences and committees and we rejoiced to welcome some of the most important international gatherings to our Edinburgh headquarters.

UBS COUNCIL – CHIANG MAI

It was therefore with confidence and justifiable satisfaction that Fergus Macdonald, our Chairman at the time, and myself set off in 1980 to attend the meeting of the United Bible Societies Council to be held in Chiang Mai in Thailand. It was great to reflect that it was eight years since I had started my work in the Bible Society movement by attending the Council meeting in Addis Ababa. The theme of this occasion was to be 'God's Word, Open for all.' The sheer size and urgency of the situation was summed up in the announcement that an estimated two billion people remained unreached by the Gospel. This challenge and the resources that would be required to meet it were constantly in the discussions and prayers of the Bible Society leaders in Chiang Mai.

But beyond the figures and the calculations was the sense of the presence and the purpose of God. It is His will that His word should be open for all. In the Bible Studies that were taken by the Rev Donald Coggan, President of the United Bible Societies and former Archbishop of Canterbury, there was joy and expectation. Commenting on verse 2 of chapter 2 of Paul's letter to Timothy – 'The Word of God is not shut up', Dr Coggan said, 'It is interesting to see how different minds dealt with this text. It reminds us again and again, down the course of the Church's history, that nothing can change the Word of God. Nothing can stop its power, though the price paid is often that of suffering and death.'

Naturally, I was very conscious of the eight years that lay between my attending the Council in Addis Ababa and the Council in Chiang Mai. It had been an enriching period of my ministry, in touch and joint endeavour with so many wonderful people in so many parts of the world. It seemed significant that from the meetings at Chiang Mai, I should have the joy of going on to Hong Kong, to share in the thirtieth anniversary of the Hong Kong Bible Society. There I received a presentation copy of the new translation of the Bible in modern Chinese to take home to give to Mrs David McGavin, widow of the former member of the National Bible Society of Scotland staff who was the first general secretary of the Bible Society in Hong Kong. I shared fellowship there with many Chinese friends and was happy to renew my friendship with Dr Heyward Wong, General Secretary of the Hong Kong Bible Society, whom we had entertained in Scotland. He was a remarkable man, moving easily in many circles, holding doctorates in Science and Music but counting it a priceless privilege to serve the Bible Cause in Hong Kong, for the Chinese there and in mainland China.

The joy of the family

As I left for Chiang Mai, I was buoyant with hope for our family. They had been steadily proving themselves in their chosen way of life.

Peter had completed his training as an architect and was proving himself a valued member of a team of architects in the Dean Village.

Isabelle had finished with distinction her Arts Degree and Teacher Training course at Aberdeen University and began teaching in Edinburgh.

Anne was serving with great success in teaching mathematics in a sixth form college in Southport.

But now happened the amazing thing, that within eighteen months, April 1979 to September 1980, all three were to be married.

Isabelle was the first, being married to Iain Plews in St John's and King's Park Church, Dalkeith by her father. She met Iain at Aberdeen University. He was a geologist and had already started work in diamonds in South Africa, before they decided to get married. They set off with great enthusiasm for what was to prove a highly successful eight years in varied areas in gold and diamonds. Iain's father and mother were at the wedding, his father being Number One in Lyon and Turnbull, the auctioneers in Edinburgh.

Anne was to marry another teacher, Stuart Smith by name. They met at school in Southport, where Stuart was a teacher in Modern Languages. They were married in the Presbyterian Church in Preston, the city where Isa and Jim Smith lived and where Anne had been brought up by her aunt and uncle. Peter, Barbara and I had an enjoyable run south to attend the wedding and came away happy that Anne was in good hands.

Peter produced a bride from Australia. Janet Fyfe came across the world in pursuit of her studies into cystic fibrosis in children. She was to study at Edinburgh University for her doctorate. This she did with great distinction and found a husband into the bargain. The wedding was in Cranstoun Church outside Dalkeith and I performed the ceremony. We were delighted to welcome Janet's parents from Australia. The fact that Jim Fyfe was a farmer made an immediate link with Barbara.

Surprise Surprise

Almost straight from Peter's wedding, I caught the plane for Chiang Mai, so we were not wasting time in those days. Two weeks later I returned to Edinburgh and Bible House with renewed enthusiasm and expectation. It didn't quite turn out as I had expected. On my arrival, Barbara broke the news that there was a strong body of opinion that wanted to put forward my name as Moderator Designate of the General Assembly of the Church of Scotland and that Dr John Gray of Dunblane Cathedral would be in touch with me to this end. I was frankly perturbed. The previous year my name had been put forward and the vote went in favour of my good friend, Bill Johnston, of Colinton. I thought it had been made clear that I would not allow my name to be raised again. But the pressure from so many whose judgement I trusted prevailed and that very month, I found myself unanimously nominated. It was a daunting prospect, though also a signal honour. The months between October and the General Assembly in May 1981 were full of planning and preparation.

I consulted with the Board of the Bible Society and offered to resign as General secretary. They would not hear of it. They believed it could work to the advantage of the Bible Society to have its General Secretary as Moderator of the General Assembly. They were prepared to accept my resignation at the end of my moderatorial year and to bridge the gap and ensure that I was fully free to discharge my duties as Moderator, they appointed the Rev Fergus Mcdonald as Colleague and Successor. It was a happy outcome, for me, for Fergus and for the Society.

Chapter 10

Moderator

They keep repeating that this is the highest honour that the Church can confer upon any of its ministers. It is indeed. The appointment is for one year, which is very wise. The pressure could not really be maintained, in absence from one's regular ministry or service for a longer period. It is also wise, of course, in protecting the holder of the office from being too carried away by any sense of his own importance. At the end of the year, he speedily discovers the reality of equality in the ministry, but goes on, conscious that something very special had happened in his life.

Another aspect of the one year spell is that it ensures for the Church an opportunity to be conscious each year of a new area of ministry, as reflected in the person and service of the person nominated. Looking back over the years, there's a wonderful variety displayed in the succeeding holders of the office that should make the Church freshly aware of the scope of its ministry and mission.

Personally, the nomination is a great thrill, bringing home very vividly the many friends one has made over the years and their concern for you. So in the provision of the equipment that a Moderator needs, I was deeply moved by the presentation of the Moderator's gown by my former congregation at Dalkeith. I was cheered to receive a stock or backless waistcoat from the Church of Central Africa in

Malawi, a reminder of their continuing concern for my welfare. The dress of the Moderator had been in question in recent years. I confess to being a traditionalist and have never felt awkward in the lace and breeches. You are immediately recognisable. I recall being greeted by two working-class men outside the City Chambers in Glasgow. They immediately knew who I was, gave me greetings and wished me well. I loved the wee lad in the highland school, who when asked by Barbara what he thought of the dress and whether it should be scrapped, replied with great conviction and the obvious support of his classmates: 'Oh, we must keep it. It's part of our culture.'

Voices from the past come breaking in, on the appointment. Those

Moderator.

I had known in school and college and lost touch with over the years renewed contact and conversation. Especially memorable and meaningful was the message from Betty Martin, who had taught me in Sunday School in Broomhill Church some fifty-five years before. After dealing with me in Sunday School she went off to China as a missionary, which in fact may have had a further bearing on my decision for overseas service.

Then a lady in Forth expressed a desire to see me. She had been servant to my grandmother in Carluke and remembered me coming to visit as a very small boy. She had some other more revealing and not entirely complimentary recollections of my doings way back that I shall not repeat. I was left with the impression that I must have been a bit of a handful. She was now in her eighties and we greatly enjoyed our recall of the past and our joy in the present.

There is so much preparation to be done from the day in October when you are nominated to the day in May when you assume office. The Principal Clerk at 121 George Street is of inestimable service in sorting out the diary for the year, helping to deal with the mass of invitations to the incoming Moderator. These are for special occasions in the life of the country or the Church, reminding us of the real significance of being the National Church, in the real sense of that title. It is a Church, committed in evangelism and pastoral care to the whole nation. So there are key opportunities for the Church and its spokesman, the Moderator to voice its mind on issues of the day and to highlight people and happenings that have moulded the form and development of Church or community.

So I found myself committed to officiate at the Scottish War Memorial Service at Edinburgh Castle, to represent the Church at special occasions in eventide homes at Leslie and Meigle, to address the Royal College of Physicians Tercentenary Service and the Royal College of Midwives commemoration in St Giles'. I was happy to speak in glowing terms of the outstanding service of the Very Rev

Andrew Herron, not least as Clerk to the Presbytery of Glasgow, from which he was retiring.

Royalty

On any state occasion, where the Church of Scotland is involved, it is the Moderator who acts as representative. Outstanding in my year of office was the wedding of Prince Charles and Princess Diana. I was invited to share in the marriage service in St Paul's Cathedral on 29th July 1981. I was assigned the prayer for the couple to be blessed with children – a simple prayer and one I was glad to offer.

Heavenly Father, Maker of all things, you enable us to share in your work of creation. Bless this couple, in the gift and care of children that their home may be a place of love, security and truth and their children grow up to know and love you in your Son, Jesus Christ our Lord.

Amen

Some months later, I had a phone call from one who wanted to know if my prayers were usually so speedily and fully answered, as she had just heard that Diana was about to become a mother.

It is great to note the widespread joy from all parts of the world that the Church of Scotland was found so fully at the heart of the wedding ceremony. The United Bible Societies took special pride in the fact that Dr Coggan, President of the United Bible Societies and myself, another prominent Bible Society figure should take part in the service, that was shared in by countless millions throughout the world.

It was a memorable service for all. The glorious setting of St Paul's, the choice music in voluntary, the singing of Kiri Te Kanawa and the congregational praise all highlighted the simple centrepiece, where two young people committed themselves to each other and to God for the fulfilment of their own lives and for the exercise of a ministry for the nation and for the world. It was all deeply moving.

London went wild that day. Barbara and I recall driving up through the cheering crowds on our way to the cathedral. It was just impossible for Barbara to resist the temptation to give a 'royal' wave of the hand to the excited bystanders. They didn't know who we were but they loved it and we were all part of a great occasion. Later that same day, Barbara and I, bereft of all our finery, went to have a cup of tea in a cafe in Piccadilly. By way of greeting us, the waitress said, 'You'd be watching the Royal Wedding on television today.' We replied that we had not watched it and then, realising she might think we were some strange anti-royalist revolutionaries, we explained why. She said 'How exciting' – and returned a few minutes later with champagne, 'with the compliments of the management.' It was just another sign of the kind of day it was.

We had many opportunities of contact with the Royal Family that year, all of them very personal and very gracious. Early on, I had to lead a delegation of the General Assembly to present a loyal message to Her Majesty on the occasion of the engagement of the heir to the throne. It was a formal occasion and I succeeded in completing the required number of steps forward and later, in reverse, without mishap. But in between, the exchanges in conversation were all warm-hearted and gracious. The Duke of Edinburgh shook hands as I took leave of him, saying, with a twinkle in the eye: 'Don't forget to turn up for the wedding.'

The reception at Buckingham Palace at the time of the Royal Wedding, when we were two among over 3,000 guests, was an incredible experience. We saw at close quarters all the members of the Royal Family. We were close to many figures in national life. It was great to meet some of those with whom we had had contact in our African days, like Lord Home and Lord Dalhousie. We found ourselves taken in charge by no less a person than the Duke of Edinburgh, who introduced us to a group of very senior Anglican dignitaries, with the comment: 'I just thought you should have the chance to meet a real Presbyterian, the Moderator of the General Assembly.'

My most memorable time with the Royals was at Balmoral, on the occasion, when, as the Moderator usually does, I preached in Crathie Kirk. When I arrived at Balmoral, I learned there was a special significance in my being there that particular weekend. Apparently, Charles and Diana had indicated they would like the Moderator, who had taken part in their wedding to be at Balmoral on the day they returned from their honeymoon. So there they were and there was I, enjoying every minute of it, deeply impressed by the warm informal atmosphere at the castle. On the Saturday evening, the Duke of Edinburgh and the Princes Andrew and Edward were out at some occasion on the estate, so that I found myself sitting at dinner with just the Queen and the newlyweds. It was delightfully intimate, as they shared with mother, the experiences they had enjoyed on honeymoon. I was impressed by the sheer magnitude of the trust the Royals placed in a guest such as myself, to be so free and natural in conversation in my presence. You were accepted as a member of the family. On the Sunday evening, we had an outing to a guest house in the grounds. We travelled in Range Rovers, the Moderator being driven most expertly by the Queen. There were no members of staff present. The Duke had gone ahead and prepared the meal single-handed. The Queen told us all what our duties were and we all fitted in. There were hilarious moments and we judged ourselves to be one happy family.

I was delighted when at lunch after the service in Crathie, it was the Prince of Wales who led off discussion on the sermon, making a number of very telling comments and interpretations on what I had said.

The Royals have marvellous memories. The Queen Mother was to be at Belmont House, Meigle for the fiftieth anniversary of her opening of the eventide home there. She greeted me almost as a long lost friend, recalling how we had met as I conducted the prayers when she was installed as President of the University College of Rhodesia and Nyasaland away back in 1957. She reminded me almost to my embarrassment how at a dinner in Salisbury I had spoken of her intended visit to Nyasaland and expressed regret that she was not to visit the glorious area of Mlanje, which was so reminiscent of Scotland and where we were staying at that time. I had not seen that she would pursue the matter further, until I received a phone call from the Chief Secretary to the Nyasaland Government, asking me in no uncertain tones of disapproval what I had been saying to Her Majesty that made her demand to know why she was not visiting Mlanje.

As to the Queen, it was always a joy to meet and converse with her. She was intensely interested in our programme as Moderator and when she discovered she would be in Sri Lanka just before we were due, she promised to prepare the way for us. Later that same year, I had the usual Moderator's London season, when so many duties are packed into ten days. It so happened that the Royal Scottish Society was holding its dinner at that time and Barbara and I were invited. Following the dinner, there was to be a visit by the Queen and among other guests, we were presented to her. She beamed all over and said: 'Now last time we met, I promised to do something for you – let me think – ah yes, I was going ahead of you in Sri Lanka and promised to prepare the way for you.' We were able to assure her that she had done it most efficiently and that everything had passed off well.

London Season

Those days in London are remembered for many things. I preached in both Crown Court and St Columba's, Pont Street churches. I thrilled to the welcome and the opportunity. It was great to see so many at these services, whom we had known in former days, especially in Africa.

I was received with great warmth of friendship at Bible House and addressed the whole staff. I sought to convey something of the thrill of being Moderator. I underlined the Bible Society contacts we had achieved in the course of our travels in Britain, in Pakistan, in South India and in Sri Lanka. Barbara and I had happy contacts with the HQ staff of both the Boys' Brigade and the Girls' Brigade, organisations with which we had long standing connections.

Then there was the joy of conducting a service at Westminster for members of Parliament from both the Commons and the Lords. It was good to be in the political environment again, even though, this time, I had rather a privileged and unaligned position.

In all our engagements, we had the expert direction and counsel afforded by John Miller Scott, the minister of Crown Court Church. He was so much at home in his knowledge wherever we went.

We had a most friendly reception laid on for us by the National Westminster Bank. The Bank also put us in their debt by providing for the whole of our London visit, a limousine and a chauffeur. The latter was a man whose knowledge of London was such that however much we might get ahead or fall behind schedule, he always delivered us to our next engagement, dead on time.

Pastoral care for Scotland

This is the continuing task of the Church of Scotland and therefore an integral part of the work of the Moderator, during his year of office. There is a plan, whereby, over a period of eight or ten years, every Presbytery receives a visit from the Moderator. I was moved by the warmth of the welcome we received, by the way so many were eager to recall by name the last Moderator they had received and the sense of expectation that something might happen, could happen and should happen through this latest visit. We were given six Presbyteries, ranging all the way from Abernethy and Sutherland in the north, to Wigtown and Stranraer and South Argyll in the south, while, in between, we tackled the Presbyteries of Perth and Irvine and Kilmarnock. Each had its own character and memories.

We chose wisely to go to Abernethy and Sutherland in the month of June and enjoyed the wonderful weather and the gracious hospitality of the north of Scotland. It was new country to us and we sensed the importance of the Church in these parts and made many friendships that have endured. We developed a special feeling for Dornoch Cathedral – the beauty of the church, the growth and diversity of the congregation's life through the 750 years past and the way in which it draws the support and involvement of the whole community in these

Moderator visiting the north of Scotland.

present times. We were specially impressed by the minister, the Rev James Simpson and his wife, Helen, and this friendship has grown through the years since.

South Argyll is memorable as including Southend, which had been a favourite holiday centre for us in years past. We had great services in Campbeltown and an exciting journey by helicopter to Jura and then on to Islay. At Southend, on a visit to a farm, I had a chance to show off my skills at milking a cow but decided to stick to the ministry. I was glad that Jura had been included even with the expense of the helicopter for landing at Ardlussa, with a sheet laid out to guide the pilot. We embarked upon a tour of the island, which was characterised not so much by the large gathering at Craighouse but by halts made at the end of roads to meet the people and at crofts where we conducted family worship. We really felt thrilled to be with the people where they are in their daily work and by the homely fireside.

Islay caught our attention as we toured the churches. I was invited to speak at a funeral service in the Round Church for a local and well loved personality who had passed on. They even fitted in a few holes of golf for us on the local Machrie course. They had all kinds of plans for us, some of which did not materialise. They had planned to airlift the Moderator, in full moderatorial dress, from the deck of the lifeboat but alas, the lifeboat had been called in for a routine maintenance check just the week before. Still we did sail around in the old lifeboat which I steered without mishap.

Our departure by steamer from Port Helen for Kennacraig was special, as I had, many weeks before, been invited to fly the moderatorial pennant at the masthead all the way. I accepted, though wondering how to fulfil the invitation, realising how ridiculous the small pennant we flew on our cars would look at the masthead. The Woman's Guild came to our rescue. A member of the Guild in the Presbytery, hearing of our need, set herself to produce a pennant of the right size. So as we climbed the ladder to the ship's bridge, to be greeted by the Captain, our pennant broke from the masthead – a joyous and proud moment. We had a further surprise, when the Captain expressed sympathy for the loss of our dear friend, Mary Lowe at Kames. We looked bewildered: how did he know? Then he disclosed that his wife had a shop at Tighnabruaich and when we were going to spend a weekend with Miss Lowe, he was responsible for delivering the chicken for our Sunday lunch. What a joy to find links established in this intimate and caring way.

Perth was a demanding area. It took ten days, as there had been a readjustment of Presbytery boundaries. So many were the requests for a visit that Barbara and I separated for periods, each carrying out our own assignment to the great joy of the people and ourselves. We visited schools, hospitals and churches. It was interesting, some years later, when I had a heart attack and was taken from Pitlochry to Perth Royal Infirmary, to be greeted by the sister in charge with the welcome 'But you've been here before. You visited us as Moderator.' So I know it from two angles.

Wigtown and Stranraer set us fresh problems, as on some days we struggled through the snow to keep engagements. All in all, it was a memorable ten days, taking us to areas where we had spent holidays and ever under the caring and watchful eye of the Presbytery Clerk, a great soul called Ron Farquhar.

Visiting Irvine and Kilmarnock Presbytery, I had a great service at Stewarton and an amazing rally of the Woman's Guild in Kilmarnock. We had an abundance of school events, of sharing in activities at the Irvine Sports Centre, where I flung bowls in full moderatorial dress. But this was the one place where my days were woefully interrupted by illness. I lay at the Fullarton Manse at Irvine, cared for on every side, while Barbara sallied forth to carry out engagements that I could not tackle. I had so many expressions of concern for my well-being that I opened a letter that arrived, fully expecting a happy get-well message. Alas, it was from Pastor Glass of the Twentieth Century

Moderator's Lady.

Reformation Church. He had been a problem to me since I came into the Presbytery. It all stemmed from a reply I gave when asked by the Press of my view of the intended visit of the Pope to Scotland. I had said that as a pastoral visit to his own people, it was to be welcomed and should not be seen as a threat to anyone else. Pastor Glass took a different view and his card was to assure me that my present illness was the direct result of my deplorable reaction to the Papal visit. Ah well, it takes all kinds! – but I deplored and I do deplore his narrow, destructive and ungracious contribution to the proclamation of the Gospel in Scotland.

In all the Presbyteries, I made it plain that I would welcome sitting down informally with fifth and sixth year pupils to invite their questions. This was done and proved most fruitful. They certainly did not stand in awe of the Moderator. They were polite but most pertinent and even searching in their questions. They were certainly not ignorant of the Scriptures, as they quoted and asked what it meant. They were alive to the world they lived in and wanted to test the relevance of the Gospel to that world. They already knew something of my own story, having been well briefed by their teachers. That made it easy for me to push home the relevance of the Gospel to give life meaning, to challenging the inequalities of life and the problems of the social and political order.

I found them less amenable and convinced as to the urgency of being found within the Church. Their perplexities about the divisions in the churches, the content of worship and the silence of the churches on what they saw as very important issues came out loud and clear. These sessions were most meaningful to me and I think also to them.

University occasions were a particular joy. What a thrill to return to my old University of Glasgow and preach in the Memorial Chapel, where so many years before I had sat as a student. The wife of the Principal had a wonderful gift of being able to identify by name the hundreds with whom she came in contact. The reception for us was special in that the Principal and his wife had avoided most of the learned and prestigious members of the University community and decreed that the young should be in great prominence, representatives of all the varied societies and associations on the campus. Ten years later, when Barbara went to consult a specialist in Perth, she was astonished to be told they had met before, at this reception at Glasgow University.

I was also privileged to preach at St Andrews and Aberdeen Universities and had also a service in Glasgow Cathedral for the Strathclyde University.

Amid all the invitations, it was specially pleasing to find room to revisit places that had special meaning for me in my life. So I went to Kirkton Church in Carluke, where I had been born. Kirkton was not the church in which I had been baptised. That was St John's but both St John's and St Andrew's sent large delegations to the service and I felt really received back home, after the many years of adventure and service elsewhere. There was a delightful moment when two ladies asked to see me at the service at Kirkton. They presented to me one of their prized possessions, a newspaper photograph of my father, in his appearance as a tenor soloist away back some sixty years before. That really gave me a lift.

Then I went to Stonehouse, where I had stayed three years with my elder brother, David in his first charge, while I was at Divinity College. There I had been ordained in 1938 by Hamilton Presbytery with my big brother, just three years older than myself, appointed Moderator of Presbytery just for that day.

My third choice to bring the past to life was to preach in Broomhill Church in Glasgow. There as I have indicated earlier, the whole direction of my life had been set within the challenge of the Gospel preached and the fellowship of Christ's people.

The Moderator and the Church Overseas

Each Moderator has a spell overseas, chosen for him by the Foreign Mission Committee, as it used to be called, or now by the Board of World Mission. Their choice for us was to spend over four weeks in the Church of Pakistan, the Church of South India and the Church of Sri Lanka. With all our personal overseas experience we were delighted to contemplate this new outreach into the shared life of the Church in other places. But that was not the end of the story. The Reformed Church in Hungary, with all its close historical links with the Church of Scotland sent a pressing invitation to me to visit them as Moderator. They argued that they knew me already through the work of the United Bible Societies, for I had visited them. They clinched their appeal by reminding the Church of Scotland that, despite the long connection, they had not had a visit from a Moderator in his year of office, since the Rev James Black of St George's, Edinburgh in 1938. I was commissioned to go and I gladly obeyed.

Personally responsible for the third area of Overseas visitation, I pointed out that, traditionally, the Moderator visited that place or country in which the main part of his ministry had been exercised. So I suggested a visit to Malawi, where I had spent twenty-five years. We expected an immediate joyous approval and were bitterly disappointed when it was not forthcoming. The Executive of the Board of World Mission discussed it and recommended that we should not go. There was apparently concern at the time about some of the claimed denials of human rights being demonstrated in Malawi and for which Dr Banda was being held responsible. They recalled my long-standing friendship with Dr Banda and feared that if I went there as Moderator, it would appear that the Church of Scotland was in support of the practices. I remonstrated in no uncertain terms, insisted that my objections to these practices were widely known here and in Malawi and pointed out that if I did not go, it would certainly be assumed that the Church of Scotland was in opposition to Dr Banda. I reminded them that I would be going to the Church in Malawi, with which I had a long-standing connection. I asked them to show some confidence in me and in my approach to difficult issues as I had proved in the past. I had decided to go whatever their final decision might be, but fortunately they eased off, putting it this way, that if I felt I should go, they would support me and pay my way.

Pakistan, South India and Sri Lanka

We covered all six dioceses of the Church of Pakistan, to demonstrate that the Church of Scotland was mindful of the needs and mission of the whole Church there and not just the Sialkot area with which we had historic links. All the bishops were gracious to us.

We landed at Karachi to a crowded airport, overflowing with pilgrims from Mecca. I had arranged for a light blue cassock to wear overseas, instead of the heavy dress of the Moderator, though I carried the latter with me for special occasions. I wore this blue cassock on the plane and descended the aircraft steps. The Bishop was delighted. As he put it – it was a sign to all present that a spiritual leader had arrived in their midst. It was interesting to note the attention paid to us in a predominantly Muslim State. The press interviewed us and we appeared on television.

My most memorable service in Karachi was to share with the Bishop in a confirmation service. There were ninety young people, offering themselves to Christ. It was the more striking when we remembered the background against which this was set – the stark poverty and underprivileged conditions of the 'busties', those cramped, crowded quarters in which they lived.

With Bishop Samuel, at Multan, we were in the presence of a remarkable character. He went regularly to Geneva for meetings of the World Council of Churches but nothing would induce him to accept the oft repeated invitation to join the staff there. His God-appointed place was in Pakistan.

We landed in from Karachi, hoping for a rest, only to be met with the welcome 'Just put a few things in a bag and we are off to the villages.' He rightly interpreted that we would want to be where the people were. It was fun. We bumped along village paths, visited schools and then entered the church where electricity had been installed and was now switched on for the first time. Barbara sat with the women on one side, having removed her shoes on entry. I preached and was captivated by the friendliness of the folk. We spent the night in a building that had been a dispensary. All the signs of the trade were there. It was bare and spartan but we were assured 'We knew you had been missionaries and would feel at home in this setting.' Indeed it was so. There was a great reception the next day, with folk from miles around. The whole place was gay with brightly coloured table cloths and scarves and we were sent on our way rejoicing.

In Sialkot, we were very conscious of the pioneer mission work from Scotland and the ties that closely bind us to the Church there. We toured the Diocese with the Bishop, the Rt Rev Qadir Bakhsh. One memorable visit was to a hospital, where the doctor greeted us with the news that their new born baby had been very poorly and would the Moderator please take him in his arms and bless him. This we did in joy and in faith and left a very happy family behind us. The hospital had special links with Holborn West Church, Aberdeen and we were able to assure them that we knew it well, for my elder brother, David, had been minister there.

We travelled with Bishop Qadir Bakhsh to the northern centre of Peshawar, where they were about to establish a new diocese. We should have gone by air through Rawalpindi, the capital of Pakistan, but the Bishop had other ideas. We went the long way by road. What a journey! We were tired and hot. We marvelled at the great buses –

105

Silver Bullets, they were called – and were thankful we were in a car. Peshawar had a reception party under way, in fact almost finished when we arrived, but they gladly resumed the proceedings and gave us a tremendous welcome. It is near to the Afghan border and we soon became conscious of the flow of traffic and people through the Khyber Pass, which we had no time to go and see. On the way back, we did visit a large refugee camp for the Afghans. They were in great need of help, which was being generously given by the Pakistani nation. What struck us, though, was the obvious confidence they had that this was but a temporary exile and that they would return home.

Lahore was a place of great delight to us. The Bishop, A.J. Malik, and his wife were charming. We loved the natural way she took her children off to put them to bed and read them a story. Some considerable time later, her husband went to find out why it was taking so long, only to discover that she had fallen asleep. Meantime, lots of friends in the congregation had gathered in the sitting room to greet us. The exchange was lively and warm hearted and in the midst of it all, Mrs Malik appeared, radiant and relaxed to take her due place in the festivities. We admired her superb calm and charm as she graced the proceedings.

We flew on to South India, to spend two hectic weeks there. We flew through Delhi and on to Madras, where we were carefully housed and guided by Peter and Dorothy Millar. We had connections with them, as Dorothy's father was a former General Secretary of the National Bible Society of Scotland. Peter did a marvellous job of guiding us through our engagement packed days. There were no breaks. Mornings, afternoons and evenings were filled. The schedule of happenings was tight but everyone was welcoming and gracious. We gained the impression of a church fully alive and in good missionary heart.

We started early in the morning and went through to late at night. On the way back from Kanchipuram, we were told there was just one

Moderator in Madras, South India.

more call to make. The pastor, on his motor bike, with his white cassock billowing behind him led the way and would stop at the road end that led to a church some distance off the road. The congregation would come out to meet us. There would be a brief blessing and we would be on our way. We arrived. The hurricane lamp was there. We disembarked to a rapturous welcome and then the lamp was lifted high. We moved along a winding path for some considerable time till we reached the church, where the whole congregation had been singing themselves hoarse, waiting for us. It was the end of our thoughts of a brief visit and a blessing. They hung garlands round the necks of ourselves and all the visitors. Since there were not enough garlands to go round, you just slipped it off, handed it to a small boy below the table, who proceeded to honour another guest further on. It was after 11 pm before we reached Madras, exhausted, but feeling ourselves absolutely heart and soul part of the Church in joy and gladness.

Sometimes, an occasion stands out because of the setting, as when I addressed a large youth gathering to celebrate Independence Youth Day. I was wearing my blue cassock and proceeded with those in charge up through the centre of this enormous crowd towards the platform. Suddenly my eye caught the curtain hangings behind the platform. They were the identical blue of my cassock. While it might please them locally that I had fitted in to their colour scheme, I was conscious as I rose to speak that I would, as it were, disappear from view and become a disembodied voice.

The day that I spent at the Madras Christian College stands out in recollection. I addressed the staff and planted a tree, but all the time, I was at the receiving end of so much that was greatly historical and eminently scholarly. There was a tremendous emphasis on Mission in the Church of South India and I read with rising excitement the thoughtful and challenging essays produced on Theological Priorities for the Mission of the Church and on Evangelism and Outreach in the

Church of South India.

Nine dioceses have their Gospel Bands which have regular programmes of preaching within the diocese. Some have Home Missions. They have chosen certain areas within the dioceses and do intensive evangelical and social work. Some dioceses have established mission fields outside the dioceses, some within the Church of South India and some outside. They also support missionary bodies by their prayers and by sending men and money.

Sri Lanka

The congregation of St Andrews, Colombo was a unique kind of fellowship, thanks largely to the very special quality of leadership given by the minister, the Rev Andrew Baillie and his sister.

We had the kind of arrival that makes us feel at home. We had been warned we would be met, but when we came into the air terminal, we couldn't see anyone looking remotely like a reception committee. So we went ahead and had ourselves processed through Immigration and our bags cleared through customs. Then, as we emerged into the front concourse, we were aware of a group bearing down upon us, obviously important, yet concerned and wildly apologetic. This was the reception committee who had planned that we be taken straight from the plane to the VIP lounge. Alas, they had been mistakenly informed that the plane was arriving late and so they gave us plenty of time to do the formalities ourselves. We tried to tone down their abject apologies, impressed by the fact that the party contained not only the minister but also the High Commissioner for the United Kingdom and the High Commissioner for Canada, who were both elders in the congregation. Having thus broken the ice, so to speak, we got on famously and planned our brief visit.

We were accommodated at the house of the High Commissioner

for the United Kingdom, Sir John and Lady Nicholas. He had been knighted by the Queen just shortly before, on her visit to Sri Lanka. We were so well cared for. His Excellency asked Barbara what he could do for her, to which she replied with feeling after the long journey, 'Just give me a bath.' He knew exactly what she meant, but he kept on teasing her as to when he was to be allowed to give her a bath.

We saw the many aspects of Colombo and became conscious of the very tense atmosphere prevailing between the Tamils and the Sri Lankans. We were graciously received at State House by the President of Sri Lanka in the very building where the Queen had stayed not so long before. The heat was terrific but as we prepared for a day's outing to Kandy, going by car, we were cheered by the assurance that the car was air-conditioned. It was indeed but the air-conditioning broke down and we suffered in consequence. The visit to Kandy was wonderful. We wandered about and admired the beauties of the place.

The highlight was undoubtedly our connection with the St Andrews Manse and Kirk. Martha was a most gracious hostess. We were reminded of the more spacious days of colonial rule, as we saw how many servants she had, and of her care for them. I was intrigued but not a little embarrassed when I heard how she had impressed upon them what a 'big, big' man was coming to visit.

Andrew Baillie exercised a great ministry there and made an impact on every part of the community. St Andrews was the meeting place for Christians from ever so many backgrounds. It was exactly as it described itself – international and inter-denominational. I enjoyed preaching at the service and was specially moved, when at one point, Andrew called all the children to the front of the church and invited me to bless them.

I have had occasion more than once to refer to this act of blessing, which I encountered quite often in travels in Pakistan, South India and

Sri Lanka. It is obviously an integral part of faith and obedience and means so very much to those who impart and to those who receive the blessing. I felt that, very much in this, I was fully the servant of the Lord.

The Reformed Church in Hungary

This special invitation was most welcome. I had enjoyed my contacts with Hungary as General Secretary of the National Bible Society of Scotland, had sensed the deep spiritual longing that existed in that land and had met just one or two of its distinguished citizens. Now I was in a special position of honour and responsibility. John Dobos and Bertalan Tamas, past and present pastors of the Church in Budapest were there to greet us. Soon we were introduced to the Bishops of the Reformed Church. They introduced us to different aspects of the life and work of the Church there. I was constantly made aware how close are the historical ties between the Church of Scotland and the Reformed Church in Hungary.

Our first big function was at Debrecen, where we were received by Bishop Tibor Bartha, as we visited the Reformed College. I had been invited to address those assembled on the theme of The Church of Scotland and Its Mission today. The place was crowded. There was a warmth of welcome and a sense of expectation among the hundreds of staff, students and ministers of the church and so many others. I felt deeply moved and greatly challenged. My speech was interpreted by John Pastor, who had served as a Theological Tutor at Limuru in Kenya, so that he and I had an immediate rapport.

I spoke simply of the work of a Moderator, reminding them that it was not a position of power but rather bore an ambassadorial function. There was the sheer joy of moving among the family of faith in Scotland and across the world.

I spoke of the changing pattern of ministry, the place of women in the ministry and of the evangelism so urgently needed among youth. I asked the question – to what does Youth respond? I drew the contrast between presenting the Gospel as the call to personal salvation or in terms of the urgent social and political questions of the age. I pleaded that it must not be an 'either or' approach. It would be fatal if we became so apparently this worldly that we were scarcely distinguished from Government or political parties. The Church must deepen its spiritual life. There is a spiritual exercise to be performed before practical issues can be faced.

Recalling an invitation to prayer that I made in the General Assembly of our church just before a key debate, I was very conscious of the pressure of the Spirit of God. This is necessary for the Church – not the brilliance of our theologians, though we think we have them, as in former days – not the efficiency of our administration, though there can be no room for sloppiness on the Lord's business – not an obvious identification with social, economic or political issues, but prior to and informing each and all – sensitivity to the movement of the Holy Spirit. That in itself should leave us burdened with the needs of the world, speaking in judgement and ministering in compassion.

The highlight of my visit was in the service of worship on the Sunday morning in the Budapest Scottish Mission. I had various functions to perform but the main feature was the recognition of the lifework of Jane Haining. Bishop Karoly Toth was present. Besides the regular worshippers, the large congregation included many interested people. There was the Ambassador of the United Kingdom, Brian Cartledge, with his wife and a number of the Embassy staff. The Scripture lesson was read by the Ambassador. Bishop Toth set the scene. He reviewed the 150 years of memorable history upon which the Scottish Mission looks back today.

The Mission was originally established in Pest to preach the Gospel to the Jews, but it has also given the example of missionary responsibility and unselfish service in the apocalyptic years of World War II, when this was so much needed.

He paid tribute to the memory of Jane Haining, from Glasgow, one time matron of the Scottish Mission. She was arrested by the German Secret Police on 4th April 1944 and deported to Auschwitz, where she died as a Christian martyr.

We were privileged to meet those who had been students under her care, and who, only now, thirty-six years later, learned the full story of her resistance, arrest and death. They were deeply moved and in tears as they remembered the graciousness of a teacher, and the severance from a friend. They had understood that she died from pneumonia. Now they faced the bitter truth. But there was joy in the congregation as we remembered her and fervent prayer that we might be found worthy of such a colleague. A marble tablet was unveiled in her memory.

I preached at the service. The official record refers to the sermon as follows:

In the course of the bi-lingual English alternating with Hungarian – service, Moderator Doig preached on John 15:16, 'You have not chosen me but I have chosen you that you should go and bring forth fruit.' The Moderator gave a dynamic witness to Jesus Christ, who has chosen us to be His co-workers, not as though our nature in itself, made us suited to this task but in order that His love, choosing us may give purpose to our lives and enable us to practise love, to act the love of the Gospel on this earth, among our fellow men, to their good. The loving sermon, savouring of a genuinely Calvinistic spirit was keenly followed by the congregation.

There were other rewarding and demanding engagements. We were received by President Imre Heber of the all-Hungary agency of the Hungarian Israelites and the Budapest Synagogue.

We attended a reception given by the British Ambassador. There were present leading personalities of Hungarian Church Life.

I was received by the State Secretary, Imre Mikloe, President of the State Office for Church Affairs. Our exchange of ideas and comment ranged from the nature of the Faith and the power of the Church to the problems that concern the human race and the peace of the world. It was most revealing and took me back to my visit to Poland a few years earlier, when I had met the State Secretary for Religious Affairs in Warsaw. In both cases, I was conscious most of all of the spiritual awareness and concern for others that shone out so clearly from both men, who were so lightly labelled as atheists.

Malawi

We had planned it all and it all went according to plan. Indeed the outcome far exceeded all our expectations. We began with two weeks' holiday in South Africa with Isabelle and Iain at Vryburg. Then we took them with us on the Moderator's tour of Malawi, arriving on Thursday 8th April 1982. Barbara and I were received as VIPs and Isabelle and Iain were taken further along the immigration counter to check in. There broke out from that end, excited cries and joyful celebration. The immigration officers had discovered that Isabelle was born in Malawi and at once she became the VIP. Everywhere we went, our joy in being back was equalled if not exceeded by the joy of the Malawians having us among them.

At the official Synod reception for us, the Rev William Pembeleka, the senior minister, whom I had known so well through all the years of my service, recalled that I had been forty-four years an ordained minister of which I had spent twenty-five years in Malawi. 'So,' said he, 'we are met today to congratulate the Church of Scotland in having a Malawian Moderator.'

We had arrived on the day before Good Friday, so we were happily involved in all the Easter Services. I preached at the services in Blantyre Church on Good Friday – at 9 am in Cewa, and at 10.30 in English. Though a bit nervous, I was amazed to find how the Cewa language came back to me, as I preached and I could not have wished for a more attentive and responsive congregation. The volume and joy of African singing overwhelmed us and we felt really back home in Malawi.

They told me later that they had great discussions about appointing an interpreter, to help me to get my message across. After all, they had reasoned he has been away for twenty years. They decided not to appoint the interpreter and said they were relieved beyond measure when they heard the sermon unfold.

We had a delightful function to fulfil after the service, when we

Blantyre Church, Malawi.

presented a suitably inscribed Communion Wine flask from the congregation of St John's and King's Park, Dalkeith to the congregation at Blantyre, Malawi. The connection had come alive in recent times, as two members from Dalkeith served the Blantyre Synod. They were Margaret Galbraith and Elspeth Dougall. It was also singularly appropriate that I, who had been minister at Blantyre before I became minister in Dalkeith should, as Moderator, seal the living connection between the two congregations. It gives a lively meaning to the understanding of the faith we share and the reality of the world Church.

We stood around after the services and met so many old friends. Isabelle and Iain were not allowed to feel the least bit out of it, as so many gathered round to greet them and to remind Isabelle of days past. Isabelle and Iain from the very start entered into everything with interest and enthusiasm. We arranged for Isabelle and Iain to hire a car to get them round, independently of us, if they wished. They even got a big discount on the hiring charge, because of the moderatorial connection.

The Saturday was a full day as we visited the Sangayas and recalled former days with Mrs Sangaya, the widow of our General Secretary, colleague of former days. Then we went on to Chancellor College and the Theological College at Zomba, afternoon tea with friends at Zomba Mission, and then, up the mountain to spend the night at the Church cottage on the Cewa, rebuilt from our days at Zomba but still on the very edge of the mountain with its magnificent outlook across the Zomba and Phalombe plains.

We were up early the next day (Easter Sunday) at 5 am, at least Barbara and I were up and ready for off on the long two-hour run by bus to Mangoche (Fort Johnston as we knew it of old) where the prayer house I remembered was now a fully fledged church. The bus was full with the choir from Zomba, clad in their official outfit. They sang all the way and yet had voices left to lead the singing at Mangoche.

Isabelle and Iain took their time and followed in their hired car, arriving half-way through the service to a joyous welcome. It was a thrill to preach the Easter Message in that particular place, a thriving and eagerly witnessing congregation in an area that is predominantly Muslim. I felt proud of the Synod that out of all the large and important centres to which they might have sent us, they chose to give us the joy of Easter to share with this small and developing fellowship. They were so gracious in their welcome and so sad at our departing, as we faced the long haul back to Blantyre, on the way to visit the Church of Central Africa Presbyterian, in the north, beginning at Mzuzu.

Through our years in Malawi we had been up several times and become increasingly appreciative of the quality of life and intellect in the north. This time we spent just six days in the area but our hosts filled the days with engagements and warm hospitality. They gave Isabelle and Iain a car to tour across to Nkata Bay. They were warned to take some food as supplies might be scarce. They arrived at a guest house in Nkata Bay, were courteously received and given a room. The proprietor took their passports for registration purposes but returned almost immediately, beaming all over. Isabelle was the daughter of Bambo Doig. She was born in Malawi. She was most welcome. Come there is a better room available for you. So, again, they were the VIPs, though the man did not miss his chance when they were leaving, to suggest they might like to leave behind the extra food they carried, for indeed things were in short supply. Gladly they passed over the items requested and everyone was happy.

I was conscious how fully they maintained the various aspects of witness so traditional from their past. As distinct from Blantyre, Livingstonia still plays an outstanding part in the medical work of the country, and we toured with appreciation the hospitals at Embangweni, Ekwendeni, and Livingstonia. We toured beyond Livingstonia to the bays on the way to Karonga, returning south on the Saturday, ready for a great service at Limbe, followed by another at Ndirande. We admired the site of the new church at Limbe. There was a packed congregation at Ndirande. Two visitors from Scotland, who just happened to have turned up, found themselves involved in the welcome to us and went away with a joyful story to tell of spontaneous and warm-hearted Malawian fellowship.

We left on the Thursday, parted from Isabelle and Iain at Johannesburg and continued on our way to London and Edinburgh, full of renewed energy and ready for the hectic weeks of engagements leading up to the General Assembly in May, when I would hand over my responsibilities to another.

All through his year of office, the Moderator tries to keep the Church informed of his travels, his perceptions and the lessons he has learned. I did this consistently through my year and noting that I was to be in Malawi at Easter, wrote a special article for *Life and Work* for April. I headed it 'Rejoice' and said:

> Around the world, the bells ring out this Easter and people are singing in confidence and in hope. On Easter Day, I shall be listening in Malawi but in spirit I shall sense the gladness in all the varied settings of Christian witness I have known – in Africa, Thailand, Hong Kong, Poland, Hungary and in Scotland itself. I shall preach on Easter Day in the Cewa language, very conscious of the miracle of communication of one message of hope in a multitude of languages.

The run up to the Assembly

On the last week of April, the women's meetings are held in the Assembly Hall. There are four – one for the Woman's Guild, one for Overseas Work, one for Home Mission and one for Social Responsibility. The Moderator always addresses the Guild Rally and one other meeting. In my year it was the turn of the Social Responsibility meeting to have the Moderator.

The Overseas Department, however, thought it inconceivable that after my long period of service overseas, I should not honour them with my presence. Then the Home Mission made the plea that as a member of the Home Board I could not but favour them with an official visit. I finished up addressing all four, probably the only Moderator to have done so.

That same week was the Annual Meeting of the National Bible Society of Scotland. I attended it and gave warm greetings and encouragement from the Moderator. Then, I changed my hat, so to speak, and appeared as General Secretary of the Society, submitting my report on the year's work. This would be my last report as I would be retiring at the end of May.

Through all of the Moderator's year, he is fully reported on by press, radio and television. However, the most memorable recording of our year was supplied by the Church's own team. As the months passed we realised the pioneering expertise that the Church of Scotland possessed in its video team.

What a great fellowship they shared with us, as we travelled with them in attendance. Ian Gall, John Williams, and Anne Maxwell all knew their jobs so well. No wonder they were winning awards. They even won one with us, as they produced *Moderator* – a year in the lives of Andrew and Barbara Doig. They submitted it to the Royal Television Society under the heading Education. The film told the story of the Moderator's office, the background to public appearances and in particular our actions and thoughts as we continued on our joyful way. The film competed against formidable opposition and won first place as the Best Educational Programme in 1982. We received a mounted photograph of the Award, which occupies an honoured place in our hallway. They deserved their success. We watched them move with ease and efficiency and charm, wherever they went. Whether it was in the relaxed setting of the parishes of South Argyll, or in the gracious presence of Her Majesty the Queen Mother at Belmont Eventide Home or in the august surroundings of the Houses of Parliament, as we chatted with the Speaker of the Commons, George Thomas or the Lord Chamberlain, Lord Hailsham – in every place, they did their recording and reporting job with diligence and with brilliance.

The run up to the Assembly is important. We had to move out of the Moderator's flat in Charlotte Square to make way for our successor. The night before the Assembly is spent as guests of the Lord High Commissioner – in this case, to Barbara's great joy, Sir John Gilmour from Fife – at the Palace of Holyroodhouse. It was a thoroughly enjoyable, quiet and relaxed evening. The next day, we made our way in our official limousine for the last time to the Assembly Hall. There I constituted the Assembly, offered a brief account of my year in office, nominated my successor and then installed the Reverend Professor John Macintyre as Moderator for 1982.

I stepped down.

These are simple words, but what a change! I was very conscious of the burden of responsibility slipping away, as I was also very much aware of a great company of folk in so many parts of the world, bidding me farewell with affection and appreciation.

On the evening of that day, the retiring Moderator has to read the names of all those ministers who have passed on during the last twelve months and offer a prayer of thanksgiving. It is a deeply moving experience. So many of them were known to me. Quite a considerable number of them had been in my own year at College. I sensed afresh the honour that had been mine in that I was the only one in my year to occupy the Moderator's chair.

So there came to an end a memorable experience which I would not have missed for worlds. I went forth, enriched beyond measure in faith and vision and fellowship.

Chapter 11

In Retirement

At the end of May, we began restructuring our life. We arranged to sell the house in Craiglea Drive, where we had been so happy for ten years. We transported ourselves to Pitlochry. This was an unknown area to us but in September 1980 we had been offered by the Rev Bill Shannon a cottage in Moulin Square, should we be thinking of retiring. This cottage would be for renting as long as we needed it. Isabelle had a chance to see it at the time of Peter's wedding so we had full family support for the step. Having accepted the offer of renting the cottage, I hesitated when in October of that year, I was nominated as Moderator. What an expense in rent when for a whole year there was little chance of using the house! But such offers don't come easily in this day and age. The setting was ideal and once I had agreed with the Bible Society to retire at the end of my moderatorial year, there was everything to be said for having the future assured before the year of office started. We entered into occupancy in March 1981.

We did in fact use the cottage in April and May of that year for periods of preparation for the forthcoming General Assembly. We got fit by exploring the surrounding country, by climbing Ben y Vrackie and then, challenged by a friend that that was not even a Munro, we tackled Schiehallion and made it to the very top.

When we retired at the end of May 1982, we had fun adapting the cottage to be our very own. We put in a central heating system, with solid fuel. Years before, Moulin residents had decided not to have gas. Peter planned the re-creation of the kitchen and the bathroom and we redecorated everywhere.

We are so fortunate to have found such a place and soon made many friends locally. We were not allowed, however, to turn in upon ourselves. Our wide contacts continued and I had an abundance of invitations to preach, both in the presbytery area and throughout Scotland. It gave a further chance to assess the vitality of the Church in so many places. Anxiously, we asked questions about those areas of the Church's life which were weak or hesitant. We lamented the absence of so many young people from services. We recalled how we had established during our moderatorial year, that, among young people, there was no lack of response to the Gospel, even though they fought shy of the institutionalised Church.

Nevertheless, our visits through the churches of Scotland rejoiced our hearts. As follow-up to my year as Moderator, I was invited to share in key commemorations in the lives of many a congregation. Our engagements took us through the 750th year of the church in Fearn Abbey, the 750th year of Dornoch Cathedral, special services in Carlisle, Hamilton Old, Restalrig, Newlands South, St Columba's Stirling, Battlefield East, Palmerston Place, Irvine, Carluke, Broomhill and Daviot to mention but a few. I greatly enjoyed invitations to lead or act as Chaplain to In-service courses for the ministry of the Church in St Andrews University or at Galashiels.

We kept up our interest and involvement in the work of the Bible Society and of the Overseas Church.

A mercy mission

It is natural that one journey in our retirement years should stand out in recollection and in question and hope for the future. In 1983, I was commissioned by the Church of Scotland to pay a visit to Malawi on a mission of mercy. Among the ministers of Government in Dr Banda's Cabinet who had, some years back, fled the country in fear of their lives were Orton and Vera Chirwa. They were close friends of ours, both lawyers and people for whom we had the highest regard. It seemed a tragedy that their gifts had been denied to the growing Malawi nation. They lived their lives in exile in Zambia, ever conscious of their lasting bonds with the land of their birth and their concern for its well-being and future peace.

In 1982 they were arrested. Some say they were taken from Zambia. Some say they were over the border in Malawi. They were charged with treason and condemned to die. Public opinion in Britain rose to their support.

The Church of Scotland decided that an appeal should be made to the Life President of Malawi, the Honourable Dr H. Kamuzu Banda to have the death sentence lifted by the clemency of the President, if not by the action of the courts. It was decided that my long connection with Malawi, with the Chirwas and with Dr Banda laid upon me an obligation to undertake this Mission of Mercy. In one sense, I gladly accepted, though I was conscious of the delicacy of the venture, I was not afraid but was rather startled when the officials at the Church Offices told me they had had a visit from my son, Peter, asking them what steps they had taken to ensure my safety. They had to confess that they were taking no steps as they considered it unnecessary. I had no hand in the moves that Peter made but I valued his support through these days as he and Barbara were present at a Press conference both before I left and after I returned. Barbara had a heavy burden to carry, as she set herself to carry out speaking engagements during my absence and faced concerned enquiries as to my whereabouts and welfare.

I was distressed by the publicity given to my mission. It had been my conviction that I should be able to arrive in Malawi, unannounced, with only the request from the Church to the President to receive me and listen to what I had to say. Alas, the Church officials let the Press know what was planned. The Press naturally responded, writing it up with headlines and even offering to send a reporter with me. I am convinced that this publicity swayed the President in deciding not to receive me.

When I arrived, I was contacted by State House and advised that the President would not meet with me. Instead his Secretary would act as intermediary. A car would take me to a meeting place. It was a strange journey, through an area I knew but to a house I could not identify. The Secretary was courteous and friendly but he made it plain that the President was surprised that 'Andrew Doig, who had done so much to applaud and advance the self-determination of Malawi and its peoples, should now appear to be seeking to tell them, and not least, the President what to do.'

I put my whole visit in the context of deeply caring for the two lives at risk and of real anxiety for the reputation of Malawi and its President in the eyes of the waiting world, if they should be put to death. I was given the warm greetings of the President and the assurance that all I had said had been carefully noted and would be faithfully communicated to His Excellency. I returned to the Mission with no idea of where I had really been.

Back at the Mission, I was in for another shock. I said to the General Secretary that I would wait around for a few days and see what happened and that meantime, I would go and visit some of my friends in Malawi. He smiled but shook his head before uttering the chilling words, 'No, no; you are known to be here. It is known for what purpose you are here. You would be well advised to take the next plane out of Malawi.'

For the first time, I felt some fear and recalled Peter's concern on my behalf. It made me aware of the extreme forces at work in

Malawi, which accounted for the stress and strain in the life of the country and the threat to those who seemed to question this extreme element by word or action.

I left by the next plane, realising that if I did not do so, I might place in jeopardy the safety of colleagues in the Church who had so graciously received me and given me shelter.

On my way out, I had changed planes in Johannesburg and sent off a letter to Isabelle to warn her that, if I could, I would call at Kimberley on my way home. It had not reached her by the time that I did, so I was waiting on the doorstep, unannounced when they came home. There was surprise, delight and anxious questioning as Isabelle assumed that something had happened to Mum since she was not with me. I told my story and Isabelle and Iain were warm in their sympathy and understanding, sensing my disappointment but fully convinced that I had made the right decision to leave the country when I did.

From Kimberley, I contacted Barbara by phone and learned that in the absence of daily dispatches, which would have been impossible, some papers had started a story about Doig being missing. I arranged to return home as soon as possible and faced a large Press Conference at Turnhouse Airport, chaired by the Overseas Council Chairman. Peter and Barbara were there and so it was in a public hearing that I had to convey to them where I had been and what I had done. Needless to say, there were other comments and reminiscences for their ears alone, later on. The torrent of questions from the Press gave me the chance to be frank but confident that my journey was really necessary and had not been in vain. Some time later, news came that Dr Banda had exercised clemency and that the Chirwas would live.

Following the family

The movements of our family tempted us to venture forth overseas.

We had two glorious visits to South Africa. We shared life with Isabelle and Iain at Prieska in the Northern Cape in 1984. From there we went to Umtata in the Transkei and toured the work of the Reformed Presbyterian Church of South Africa along with the Rev Sam Ngcobo, the General Secretary. We made our way then to catch up with Isabelle and Iain in Capetown for a memorable Christmas holiday. At the end of it, they returned to Prieska while we went north to Zambia, to renew contact with Chipo Moonga of the Bible Society and with hosts of Malawi exiles, like the Chokanis and the Bwanausis. We were honoured to be invited along with Church and Malawi representatives to dinner at State House by President Kaunda.

He is a remarkably human and dedicated character. I had known him years before, as he recalled in a humorous story told before dinner. He said when he was asked if he would receive the visiting ex-Moderator, he said to himself: 'Now I used to know a Doig, who was strongly with us in asserting our right to independence, but it can't be old Doig. It must be his son.' Then he added with a smile, 'But it is old Doig, not looking too old either. We welcome him.'

Our second African visit was in 1986 to see Isabelle and Iain at Welkom. Isabelle was expecting her first baby, Jessica and we were there. We enjoyed our stay, made many friends in the church, had the chance of meeting important people like mine managers and heard their positive dreams and expectations for African advancement in the mines.

Jessica arrived to our great joy. After a few weeks of lazing around, enjoying the swimming pool and the local golf course, we all set off for a holiday in the Drakensburg mountains. What a holiday! What marvellous surroundings. The unexpected happened again, when I came round the corner of the hotel building and found myself face to face with Jimmie Calder, whom I had not seen for twenty-four years when he was a member of my congregation in Blantyre. How could I forget him? It was he who handled the rescue and repair of our car,

Family group on Author's eightieth birthday
(back) Iain, Peter, Janet and Stuart (middle) Isabelle, Barbara, Author and Anne
Grandchildren Alexandra, Michael, Jessica and Victoria.

when it was stolen two days before we were due to leave Malawi for good.

Barbara and I went on to the Theological Seminary near Pietermaritsburg. I sensed the tension as we stayed with them, for the Seminary was under threat of destruction by Nkatha, the Zulu forces loyal to Chief Buthelezi. I preached in the nearby township of Mbali and was thrilled with such a large and attentive congregation. I preached by interpretation and I used the sermon I had preached in Budapest on Choice and Growth (John 15:16).

Before we left Welkom, I had the joy of baptising Jessica in the Presbyterian Church. We have four grandchildren and I have baptised them all – Victoria in Palmerston Place, Edinburgh in 1984; Jessica in Welkom in 1986; Alexandra in Melbourne, Scots Kirk in 1987 and Michael in Edinburgh, St Bernard's in 1987. Of course they all behaved perfectly.

Peter and Janet and Vikki left Scotland for Australia in 1985. We were heavy-hearted to see them go but we knew in ourselves that it was right for them. We rejoiced in the new opportunities that would open up for them there. We just couldn't wait to see them, so at the end of the following year, 1986, we made the long journey to Melbourne, staying overnight on the way, in Singapore. The house and garden at Upwey, some twenty miles from Melbourne, delighted us. We toured with them to Canberra, Ballarat and Mount Baw Baw. We rejoiced in sharing the freedom and activity of the farm at Stratford with Janet's parents. When we arrived, Jim announced that as Peter had told him I used to ride a motor bike, there was one laid on for me so that I could play my full part in herding the cattle. I'm proud to claim that I proved my prowess had not departed from me.

Through our Dornoch connection with John McKinlay, who was by then teaching in Australia, we had the use of his cottage at Macrae, in the Morningside Peninsula and greatly enjoyed our time there.

I had a great round of preaching engagements, in Melbourne, in the

Scots Kirk, and in Sydney, where I officiated two Sundays at Roseville and at Epping.

We caught up with old friends as we contacted Dr Kester Brown, son of Monteith Brown of distant Tumutumu days. Kester spent his national service leave with us in Malawi in 1954 and had often called upon us in Scotland on his visits from Australia.

We had a second visit to Peter and Janet, Vikki and Alex in 1990 and this was, if possible, more exciting than the first. We shared their interests in work and university research and accompanied them on the golf course. We made a journey to Adelaide, to see Sue Bampton (formerly Childs) whom we had known in Malawi many years before. As a family, we set off by air for Tasmania, hired an eight-seater vehicle and for a week saw the beauty and varied historical interest of the island. We spent a week at Macrae and on the way home, dropped off at Sydney where we renewed contacts with the Murrays and the Macfarlanes. I preached for Doug Murray at Roseville and felt so much at home.

Though we didn't need to make long journeys to see them, we kept through these years in close touch with Anne and Stuart. They came up to Pitlochry and we made our way to Southport.

At ease in Europe and Israel

In 1983, we decided to book a holiday by SAGA to Austria and Yugoslavia. It was marvellous. We went by bus across Europe, in the course of which we sailed down the Rhine for quite a stretch before returning to the bus and eventually reaching San Georgan. It was a delightful town. We followed the broad outline of travel planned for us, while feeling free to plan for ourselves when we wished. We heard that the tour organiser asked another passenger at the end of the whole trip, who we were, for he had not seen us on the excursions.

Actually we found it better and less expensive to plan our own outings. There was plenty to see around San Georgan. We climbed the mountains and also found our way down the hill to Lake Attersee. On one of our wanderings, we met a lady and asked for guidance. She was full of helpful information, which was not surprising since she turned out to be the head geography teacher at the local school. She disclosed that she had a holiday the following day and would be delighted to drive us around. She took us to a small town with historic connections not far from Lake Attersee. It also boasted a cathedral, the many special features of which she outlined to us. We had heard that it was also the place where *The Sound of Music* was filmed. We soon kept quiet about that, when we learned that the local people don't consider it an important incident in their calendar. After all, why bother about a passing cinema production when you have so much of living interest in the area to recall.

We went on to Yugoslavia and spent several enjoyable days on the coast and had an interesting outing to Krk before flying back to Britain.

The Holy Land

In 1984, we accepted a gracious invitation from McCabe Travel to lead a party to the Holy Land. George McCabe had succeeded me as minister of St John's and King's Park Church, Dalkeith and it was his son who started up McCabe Travel. It has been highly successful and the parties formed are indeed happy bands of pilgrims. My task was to lead worship for the party daily as we moved from centre to centre of historic interest with biblical connection. I had set out with some misgivings, having wondered if the tour operators in Israel were not in danger of commercialising what should be a spiritual experience. My fears were soon set to rest as we travelled through Jerusalem, Jericho,

Tiberias, Nazareth and Bethlehem. Places came alive and words and incidents came home with fresh impact.

It was a joy to preach on Easter Day in the Scots Church, Jerusalem, sharing the service with the minister, the Rev Dr Robert Craig. I had maintained a lively connection with him through the years since I left Central Africa. He it was, as Principal of the University College at Salisbury, who kept me informed on how things were going in the College, whose inception I had helped to establish many years before. The church in Jerusalem was full to capacity. There were folk there from every part of the world. It was a joy to listen to the strong Fife accent of Bob Craig and to stand with him later, greeting the congregation as they dispersed. There was an amusing incident. Bob had suggested that for Easter Day, we should both wear our doctorate robes, and this we did. As the folk left the church, one lady commented, 'It is grand to see you both in your doctorate robes. It is just a pity that the colours somewhat clash.' I suppose the strong scarlet of Glasgow and the purple of St Andrews just didn't match! Ah well, you can't win them all.

Another memorable occasion was when I conducted a Communion service in the small chapel at the fields of Bethlehem. We were a small company, singing with joy:

> I cannot tell why He whom angels worship,
> Should set His love upon the sons of men'

to the tune of the Londonderry Air. Suddenly, the church filled up with a joyous crowd who joined in enthusiastically. It turned out that the party, from Ireland, were strolling along quietly, when they could not believe their ears as the strains of the Londonderry Air hit them. They joined us and we shared Celtic fellowship in the Holy Land.

Spanning the years

It is amazing and exciting how people renew acquaintance after a gap of very many years. Two recent examples come to mind.

A letter arrived in 1992 from Walter Chalmers of Edinburgh. He made the contact after a letter I had written appeared in the Scotsman. He stressed that he was not wanting to deal with the contents of the letter but rather to remind me that we had met long ago. He hailed me as his Army Chaplain in Kenya nearly fifty years ago. Apparently I also examined him in the Chinyanja language and to his great delight had given him a pass.

Then, in August 1995, I was invited to conduct a wedding in Blairgowrie. For both Fiona Kain and Charles Duthie, it was a second marriage and a very joyous occasion. The excitement for me was that Fiona had been baptised by me as a baby fifty-five years before, in the church at Zomba, Nyasaland, where I was minister. Her parents, Mr and Mrs Kain were faithful members. Mr Kain was a prominent member of the Government Administration. The wedding took place on a very hot day, in the hotel grounds and so it was easy to think back to our former African connection.

So the story is told. It is indeed PEOPLE THAT COUNT.

What more can I say? Perhaps use the words of the Chorus

> One more step along the world I go
> One more step along the world I go
> From the old things to the new
> Keep me travelling along with You
>
> And it's from the old I travel to the new
> Keep me travelling along with YOU.